NewMusicShelf

Anthology of New Music
Tenor, Vol. 1

Curated and edited by
Dennis Tobenski

Foreword by Libby Larsen

NewMusicShelf
www.newmusicshelf.com

NEWMUSICSHELF, INC.

Published in the United States of America
by NewMusicShelf, Inc.
34-29 32nd St., 3rd floor, Astoria, NY 11106
www.newmusicshelf.com

Copyright © 2018 by NewMusicShelf, Inc.

First printing 2018

All rights reserved. No part of this publication may be reproduced, stored in a retrieval system, or transmitted in any form or by any means, electronic, mechanical, photocopying, recording, or otherwise, without the prior permission of the publisher.

to Steven Shulman
"Don't worry about it."

Contents

Acknowledgments vii
Foreword by Libby Larsen ix
Introduction xi

Paul Ayres: The Salutation (2015) 1
  from The Light Walking

Chester Biscardi: At Any Given Moment (2002) 16
  from Modern Love Songs

Clint Borzoni: In the Golden Afternoon (2015) 22
  from Within the Looking Glass

Steven Burke: Inebriate of Air (2012) 29

Daniel Gilliam: Like men and women (2011) 37
  from Songs of Insects and Animals

Juliana Hall: June (1999) 39
  from The Poet's Calendar

Drew Hemenger: Her Final Show (2012) 44

Garrett Hope: Princess Stories (2009) 50
  from Somewhere, Love

Rory Wainwright Johnston: Like the dove (2015) 54
  from Nostalgia

David Leisner: Love and Friendship (1985-86) 58
  from Confiding

Lisa Neher: Tuesdays and Thursdays (2010) 64
from Snapshots

Frank J. Oteri: Prick'd (2016) 66

Gabrielle Owens: Black is the Color (2016) 70
from Three Folk Songs

Darien Shulman: If Thou'lt Be Mine (2007) 76
from Three Poems of Thomas Moore

Dennis Tobenski: John Anderson, My Jo (2005) 84
from And He'll Be Mine

Craig Urquhart: Here the Frailest Leaves of Me (1986) 90
from Leaves

Philip Wharton: Let Me Play the Fool (2014) 92
from Fools

Scott Wheeler: Night (2007) 101
from Heaven and Earth

David Wolfson: When First I Loved You (1998) 111
from Six Love Songs

Roger Zahab: River (2016) 116

About the Curator 119
About the Composers 120
Supplemental Materials 141

Foreword

Congratulations! You hold in your hands the *NewMusicShelf Anthologies of New Music*, a four-volume, curated treasure trove of 80 songs penned by your colleague composers and composed for you, singer of songs, teller of tales, bearer of our zeitgeist. Discover and prize these songs. They are yours now, in your keeping, waiting to rise on your breath and sing through your voices.

You might think of these four volumes of song as living-history - a vibrant mix of singers, collaborative instrumentalists, composers and our audiences. A wide range of the many excellent composers writing art song today are represented here. They are a community of composers who love the human voice and devote their talent and time to composing new work for it. We honor these composers through performance, of course, by singing the songs they write for us. We also must remind ourselves that we need to honor their work by respecting their need to support themselves with compensation in the form of the royalties they collect from sales of their music. We urge you to support your composers by resisting the temptation to photocopy and distribute music from these song collections. As the world becomes more and more digital, we think it essential that these collections of songs are available only in print. In the years to come we will be delighted to discover the *NewMusicShelf Anthologies of New Music* on pianos, bookshelves and music stands, but even more delighted to hear you filling the air with the sound of your singing - these songs - everywhere!

— Libby Larsen

Acknowledgments

First and always: thanks to Darien Shulman for your love and support and patience while I do crazy things like start a publishing company from nothing.

To my parents Denny & Janice for always being there, and for never discouraging me from pursuing this bizarre life as a musician.

To Cory Davis for teaching me so much about the art and science of engraving - you've been a mentor as well as a friend.

To Garrett Hope and Sean Perrin for being sounding boards in our video chats, and for helping to keep me on track, and not going down more rabbit holes than I can handle at once.

To Trudy Chan for your help and friendship, and for your involvement in the anthologies and everything else - you're fabulous!

To Laura Strickling, Megan Ihnen, and Michael Kelly for coming along on this crazy ride with me, and with such amazing enthusiasm! You've all been an incredible inspiration throughout the entire process!

To Jay Venute for your neverending encouragement.

And to everyone who submitted music to be considered for inclusion in these volumes: composers are the reason that I started this, and the driving force behind so much of what I do. We have an amazing community of musicians, and together we can make it even better and stronger!

— Dennis Tobenski

x

INTRODUCTION

This volume - and series of publications - exists to introduce performing musicians to the amazing variety of composers living and writing today. Whether you're a student, teacher, or professional, this collection was created with you in mind.

Every song is appropriate for a professional or student recital, and many songs were selected for their didactic possibilities: shifting meters, asymmetrical rhythms, various degrees of difficulty with pitch materials or non-traditional performance techniques, etc.

Across all four inaugural volumes of these anthologies, the primary criterion has been the curator's willingness to stand behind their selections: to be willing to perform and record every song, and make their selections without reservation. These are songs that singers should *know*, and should perform. These are composers that singers should *know*, and should work with.

And *you* are performers that composers should get to know and work with! We are all a part of a community that makes music, and we can only be better and stronger together.

As the creator of this series, I've had to personally define my short-, medium-, and long-term goals for the project. My short-term goal is simple: you getting to know these songs, and performing them. I stand behind every song and every composer, and hope that you find your own connection to these songs.

My medium-term goal is linked to a minor feature of these volumes: notice that underneath many of the song titles there is a bit of text: "from _____". Many of these songs are from song cycles or song sets. I encourage you to check out those cycles, as well as the composer's other vocal works! My medium-term goal? That you and your colleagues get to know more of the works by these composers than are represented here. This is a mere sliver of these composers' output, and their catalogs are worth exploring!

My long-term goal? Let's just say that I have plans....

I encourage you to look beyond the borders of the voice-type specific nature of these volumes. Many of these songs were written without gender or voice type in mind, and so are worth exploring by every singer.

— Dennis Tobenski
Founder of NewMusicShelf, and curator of this volume

commissioned by Giles and Jackie Adams
first performed by William Petter, accompanied by William Vann, January 2015

The Salutation
from the song-cycle *The Light Walking*

THOMAS TRAHERNE

PAUL AYRES
(2015)

Copyright © 2015 by Paul Ayres. All Rights Reserved.

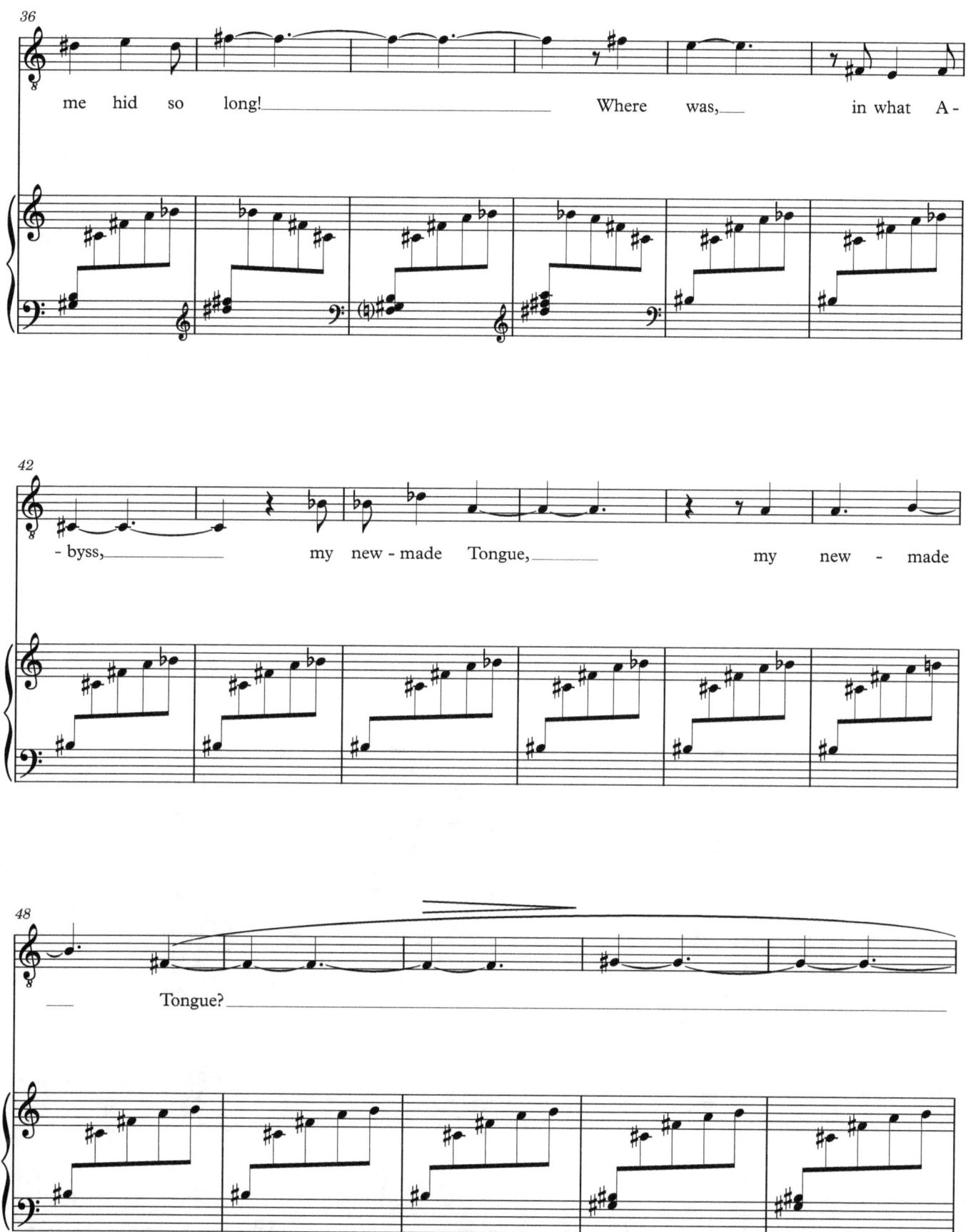

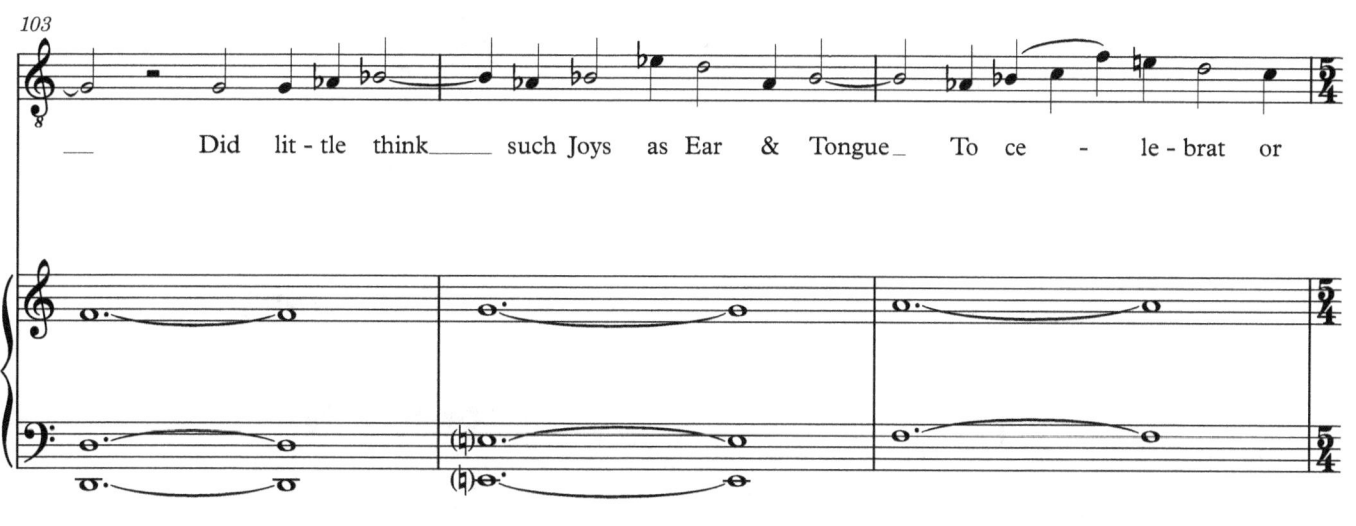
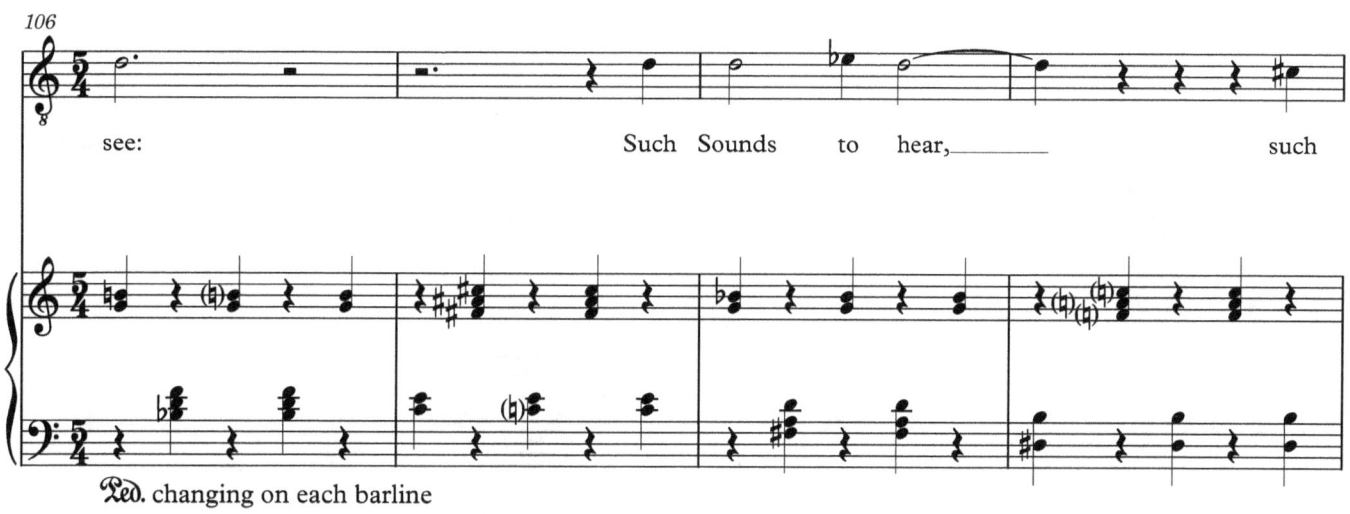
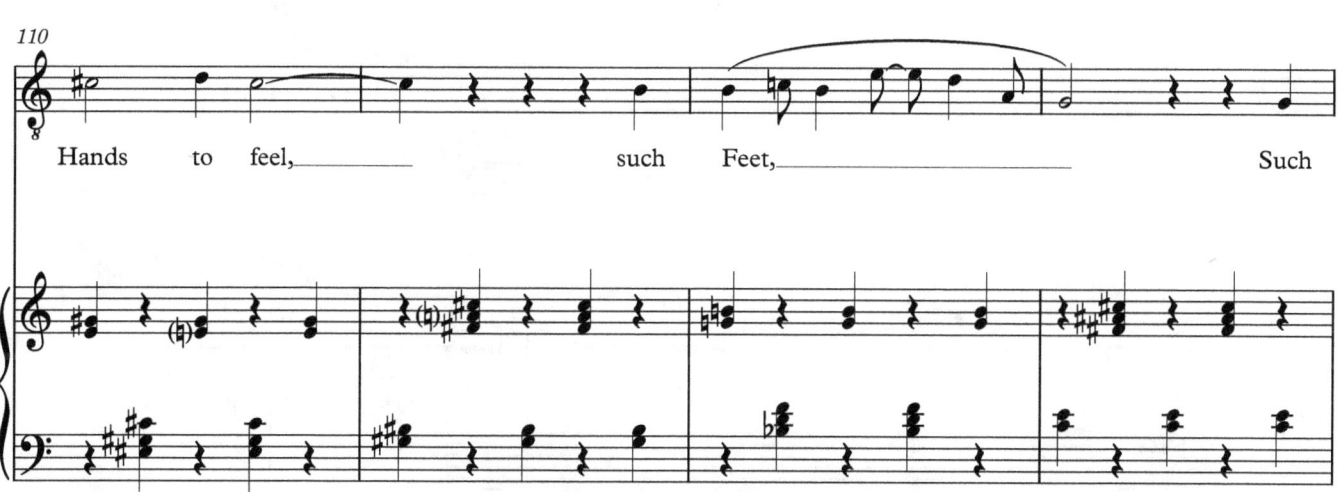

173
The Sun & Stars are mine; if these I prize.
179
p leggiero
Ped. changing on each barline
182
mp
A Stran - - - ger here

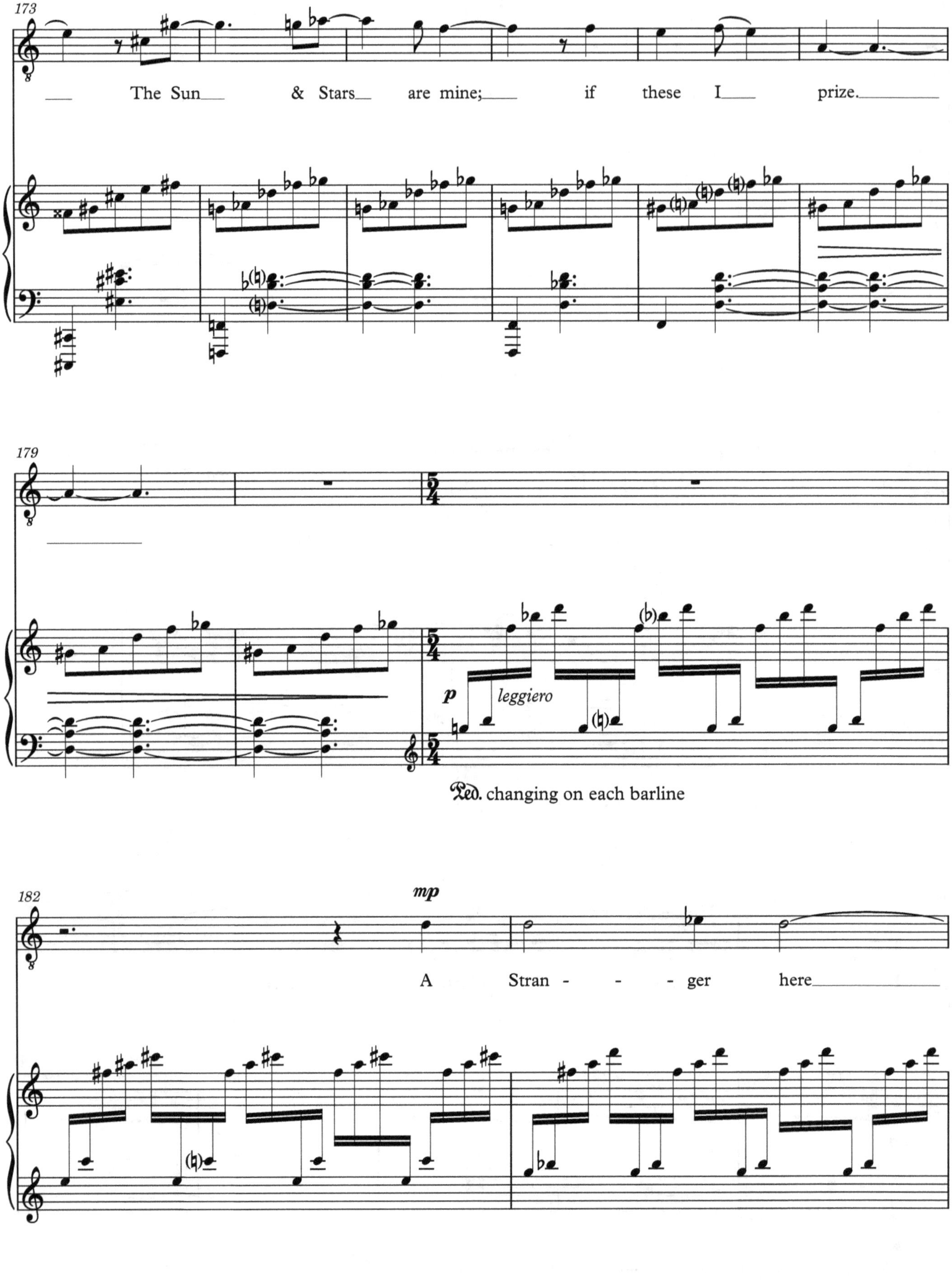

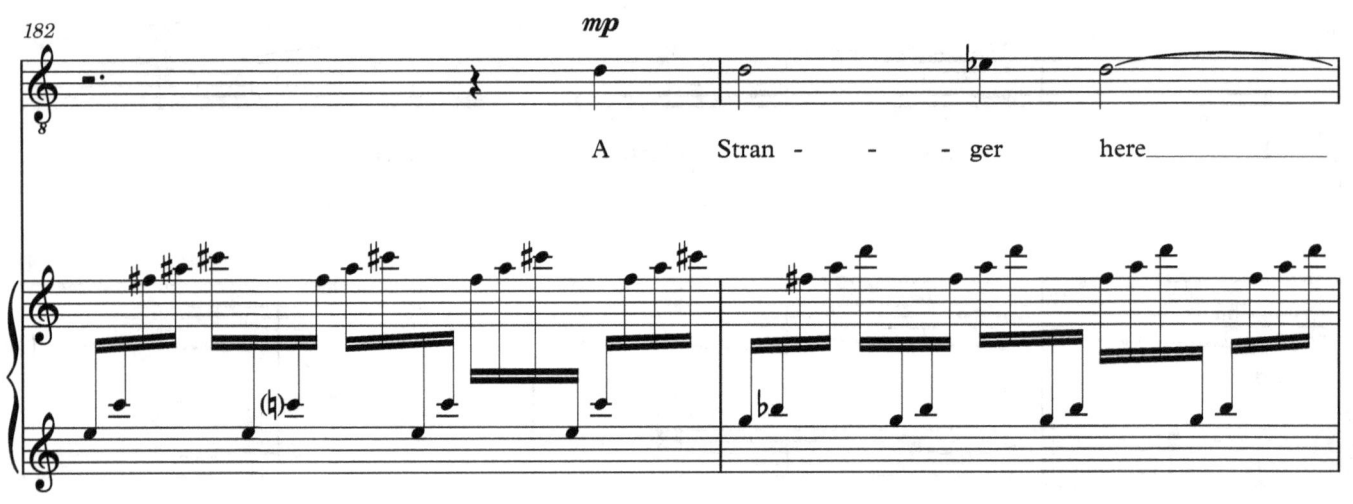

At Any Given Moment
from *Modern Love Songs*

WILLIAM ZINSSER

CHESTER BISCARDI
(2002)

Copyright © 2001. All Rights Reserved by Chester Biscardi and William Zinsser.

18

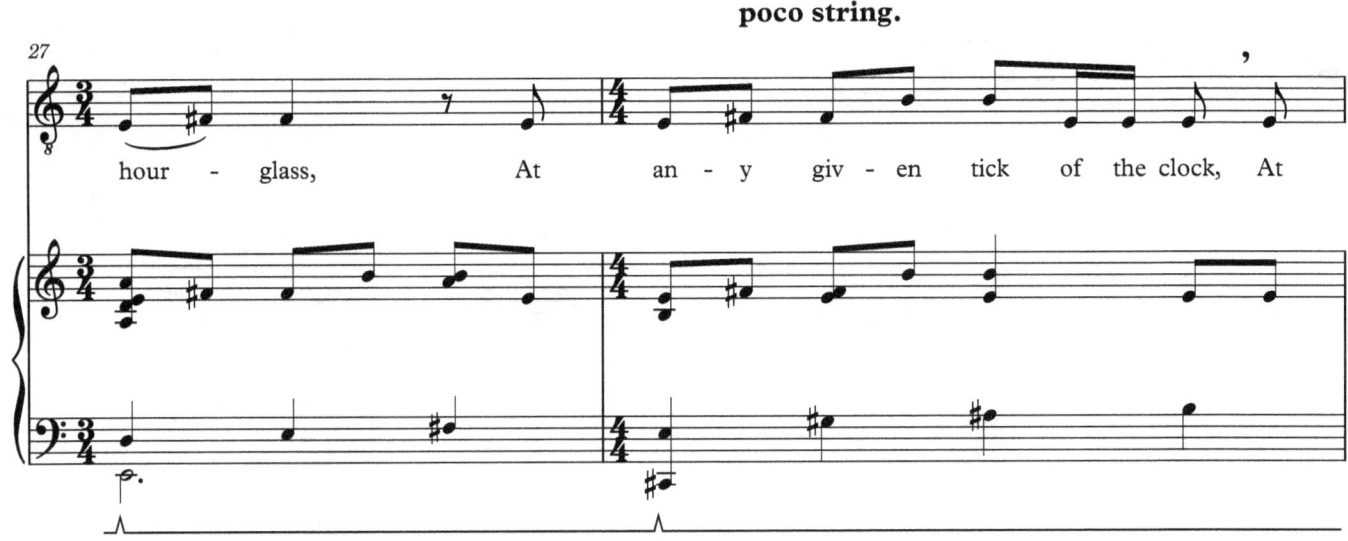

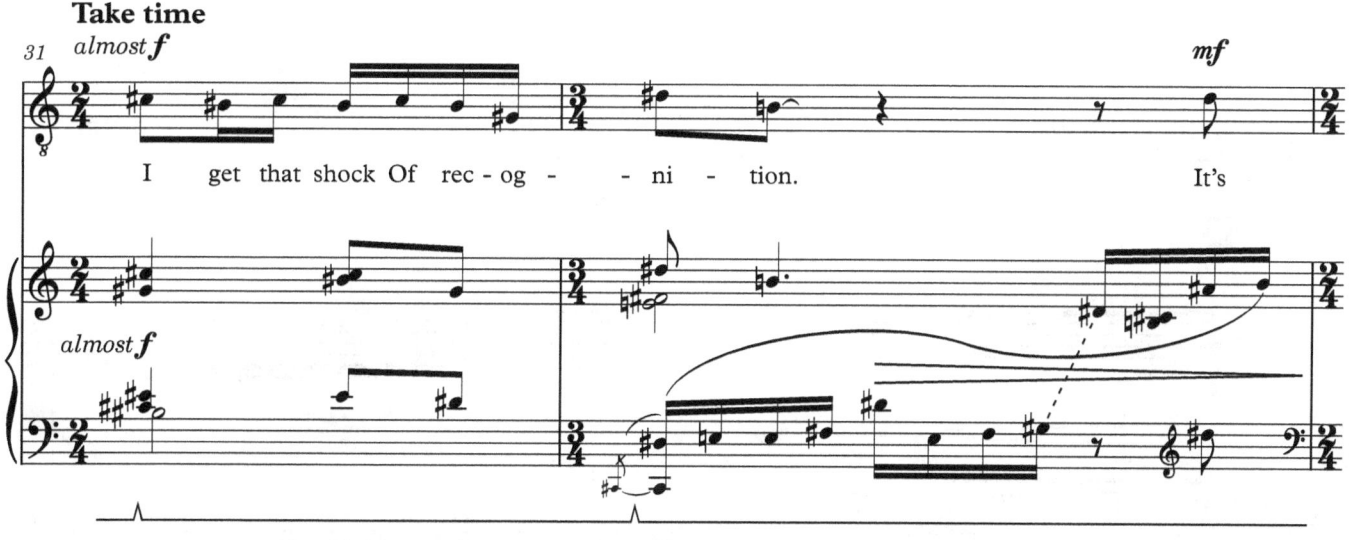

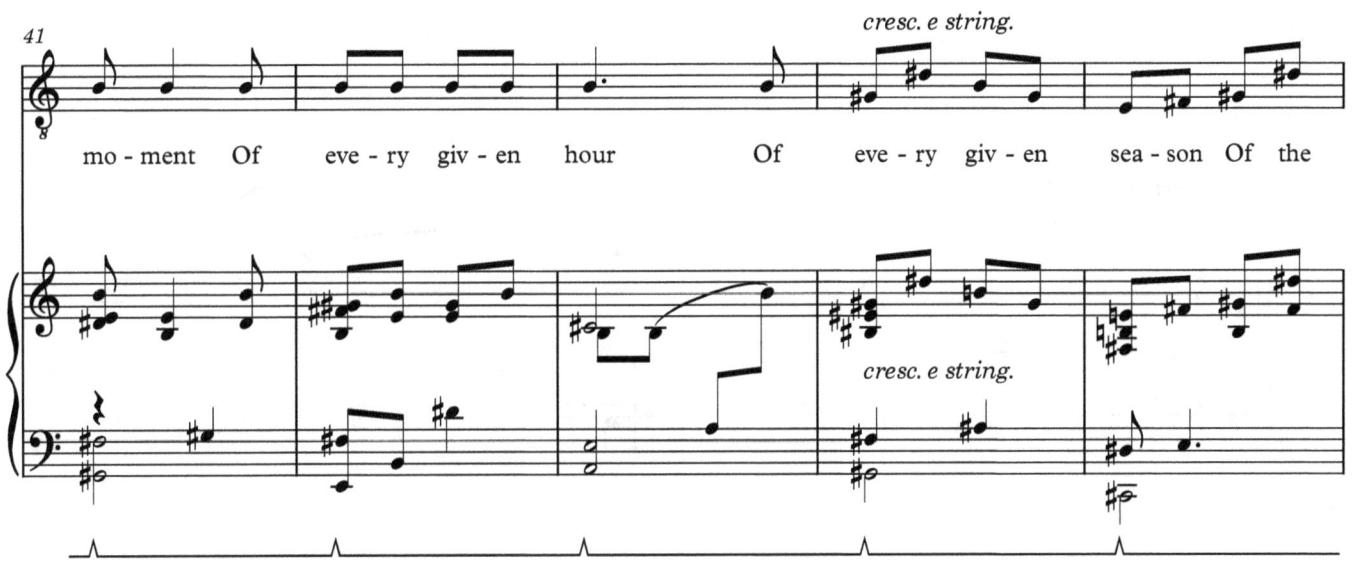

Commissioned by tenor Mitchell Sturges

In the Golden Afternoon
from *Within the Looking Glass*

LEWIS CARROLL

CLINT BORZONI
(2015)

Copyright © 2015 by Clint Borzoni. All Rights Reserved.

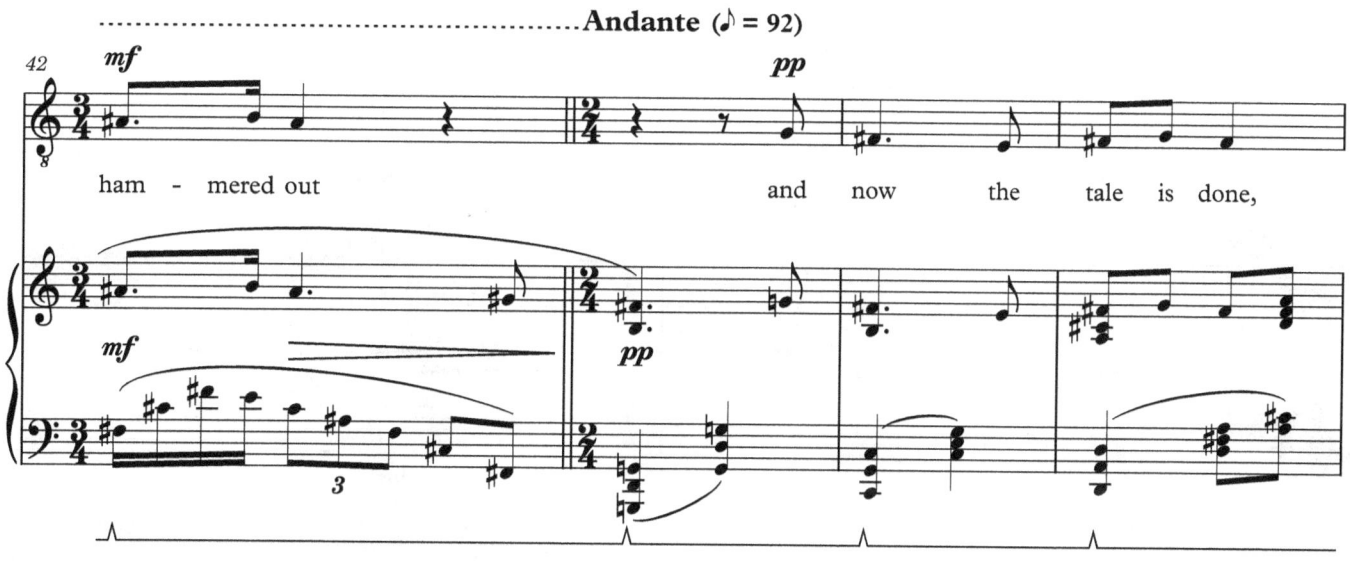

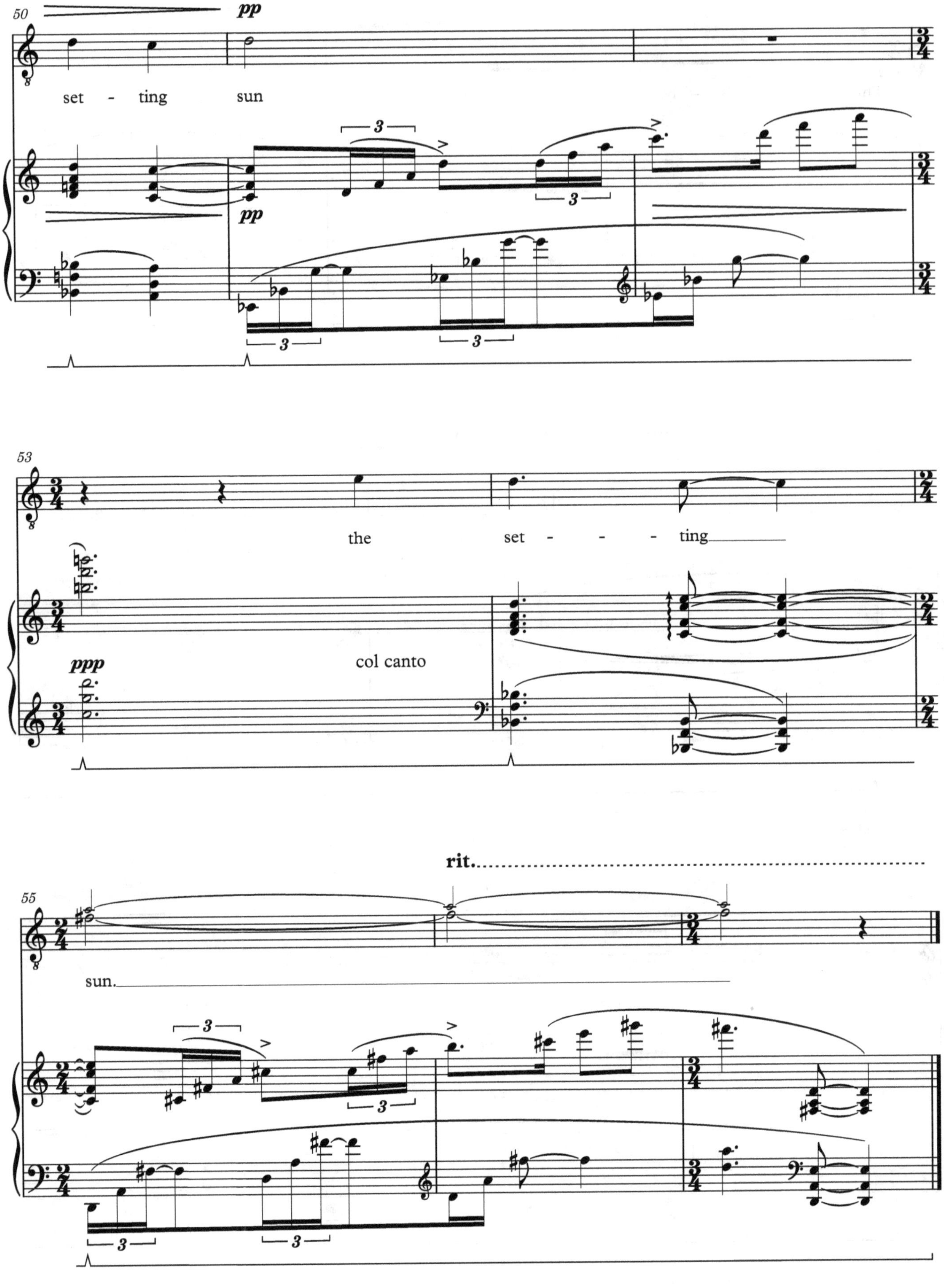
50
pp
set - ting sun
pp
53
the set - - - ting
ppp
col canto
rit.
55
sun.

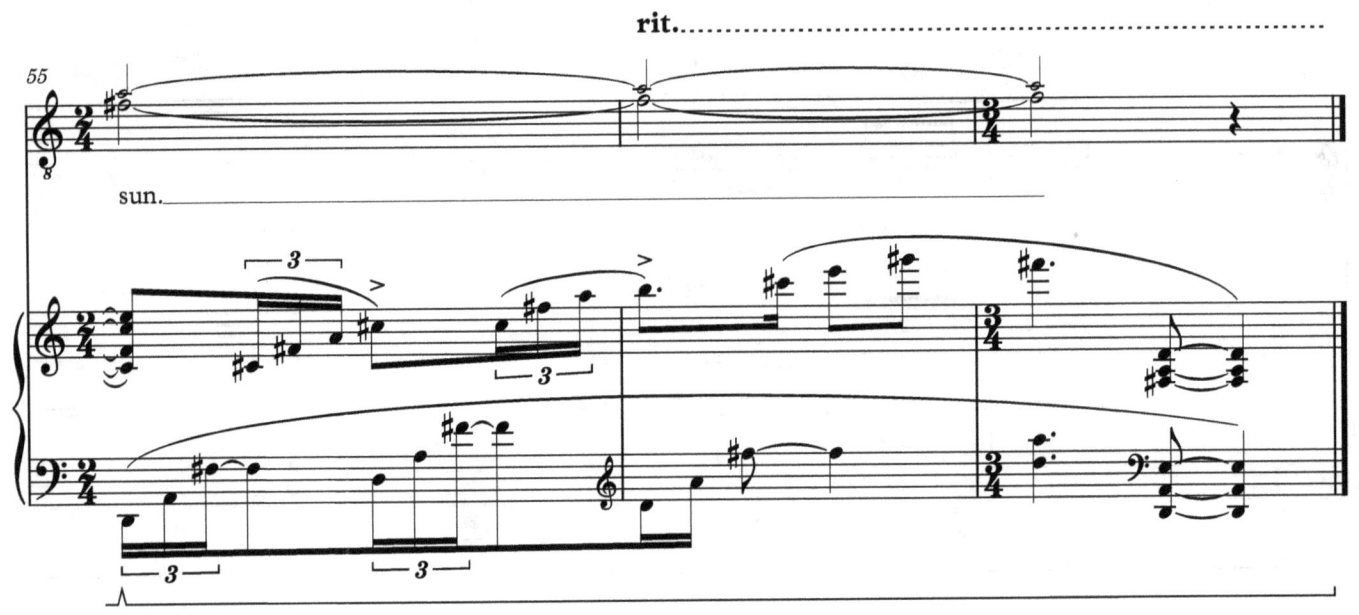

for Joseph Caldwell in loving celebration of his birthday
Inebriate of air

EMILY DICKINSON STEVEN BURKE
(2012)

Fast, nimble, effervescent ♩ = ca. 112

Copyright © Steven Burke June 2012. All Rights Reserved.

July 22, 2012
New York, NY

Like men and women
from *Songs of Insects and Animals*

EMILY DICKINSON

DANIEL GILLIAM
(2011)

Copyright © 2012 Fictive Music (ASCAP). All Rights Reserved.

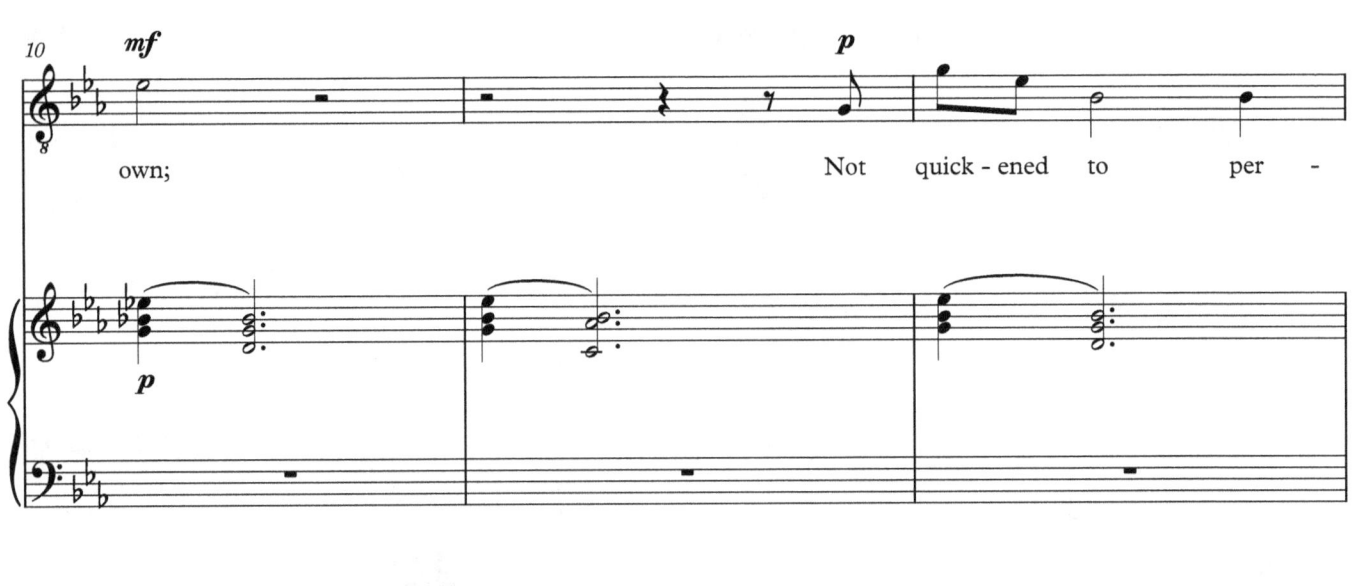

August 8, 2011

June

from *The Poet's Calendar*

HENRY WADSWORTH LONGFELLOW

JULIANA HALL
(1999)

Copyright © 1999 Juliana Hall Music. Copyright transferred 2017 to E. C. Schirmer Music Company, Inc.
Copyright © 2017 by E. C. Schirmer Music Company, Inc., a division of ECS Publishing Group. www.ecspublishing.com
All rights reserved. Used by permission.

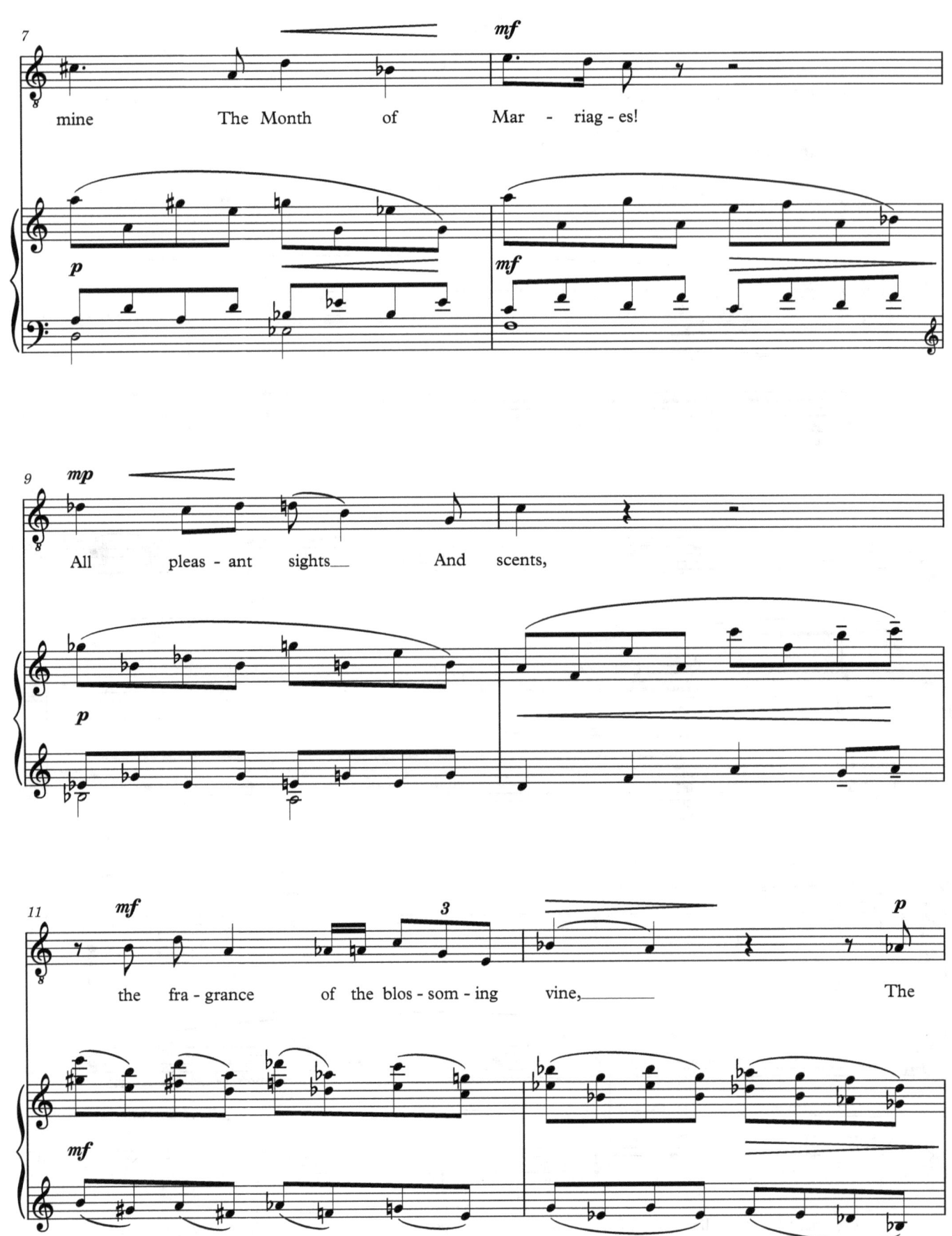

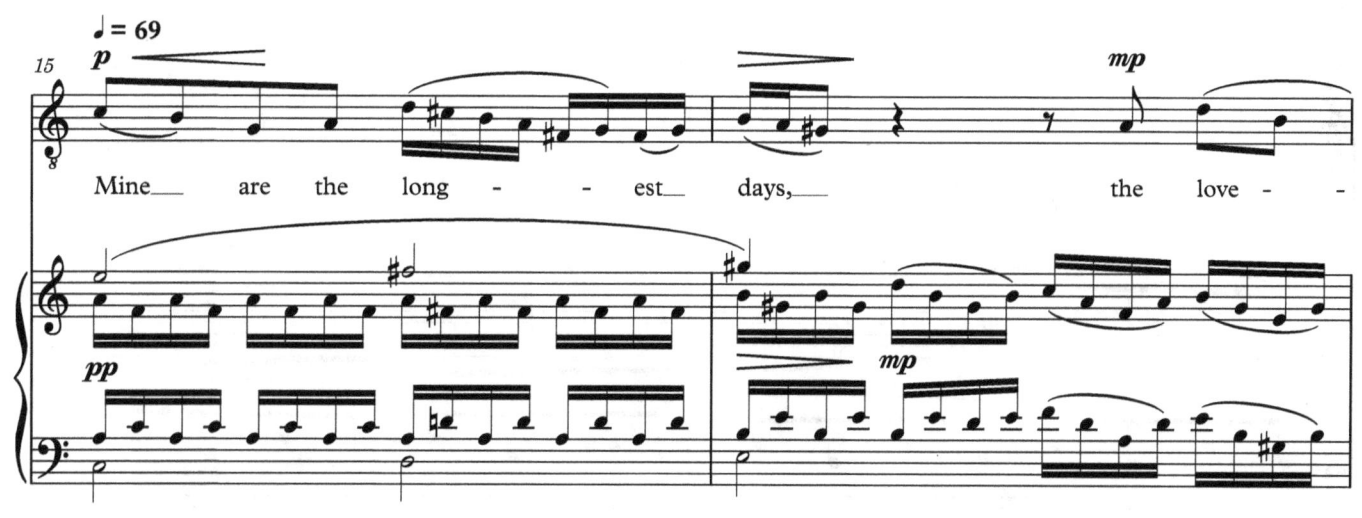

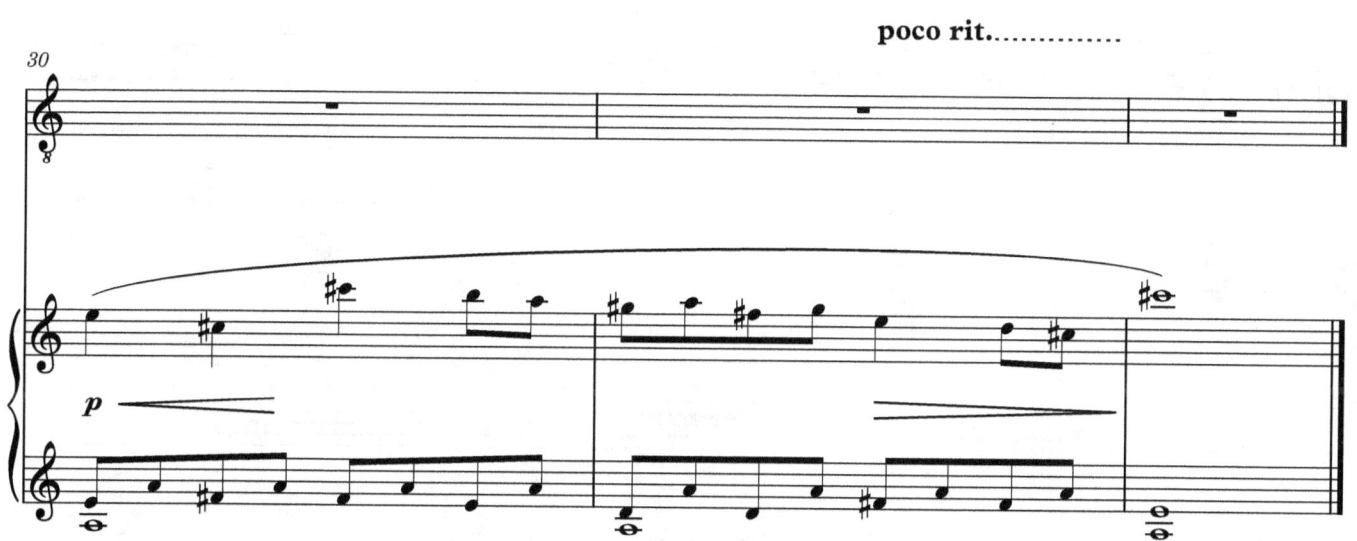

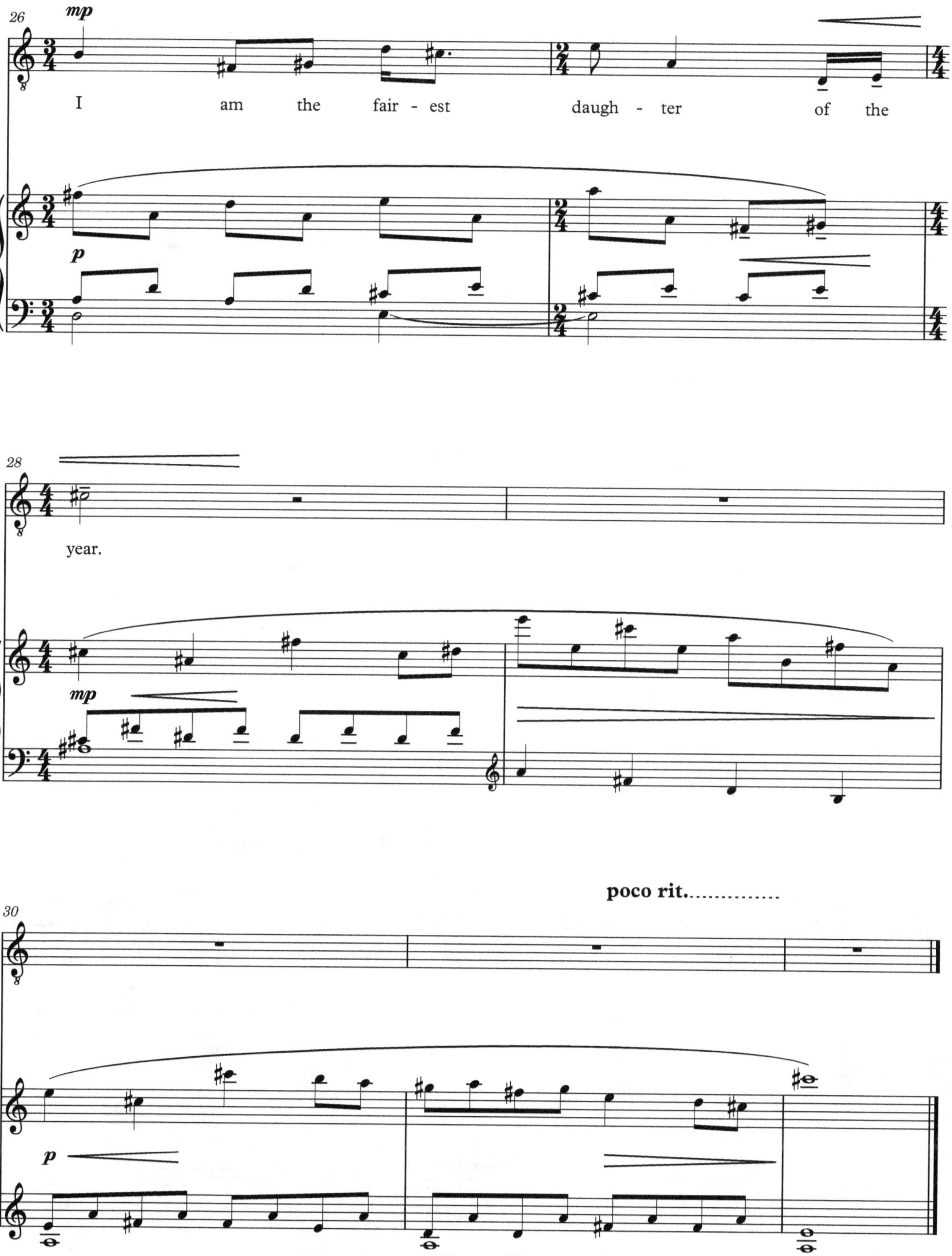
26
mp
I am the fair - est daugh - ter of the
p
28
year.
mp
30
poco rit...............
p

In memory of those who are no longer with us; in honor of those of us who, by the grace of God, fight on

Her Final Show

RAFAEL CAMPO

DREW HEMENGER
(2012)

Copyright © 2012 by Drew Hemenger. All Rights Reserved.
Text copyright © by Rafael Campo.

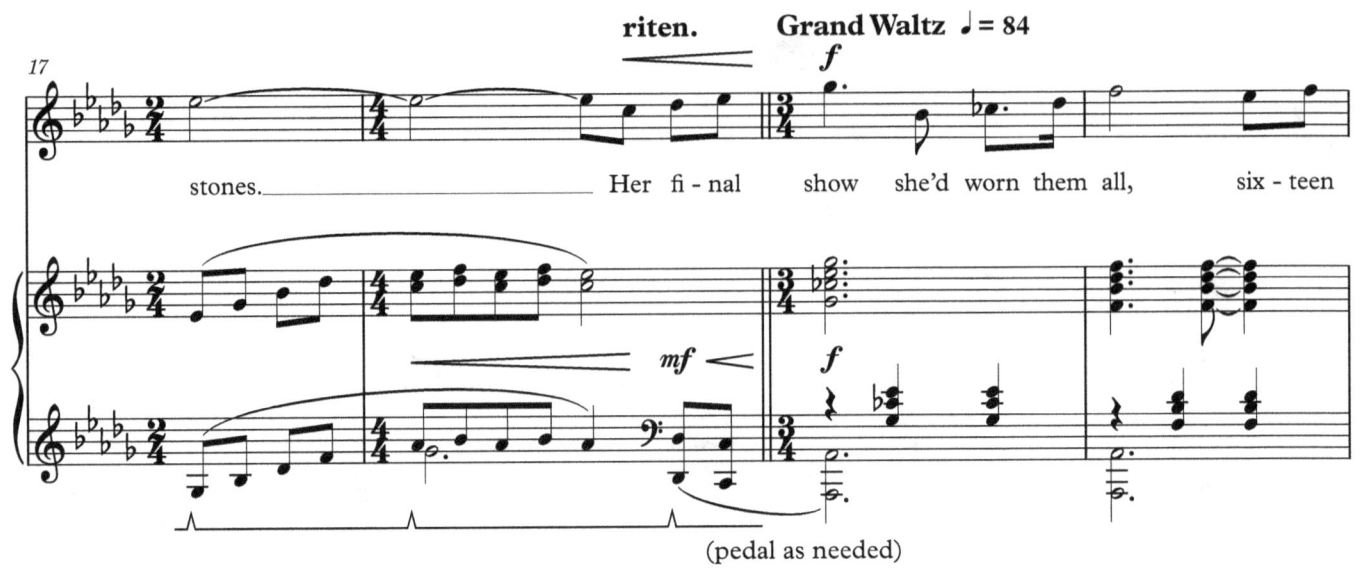

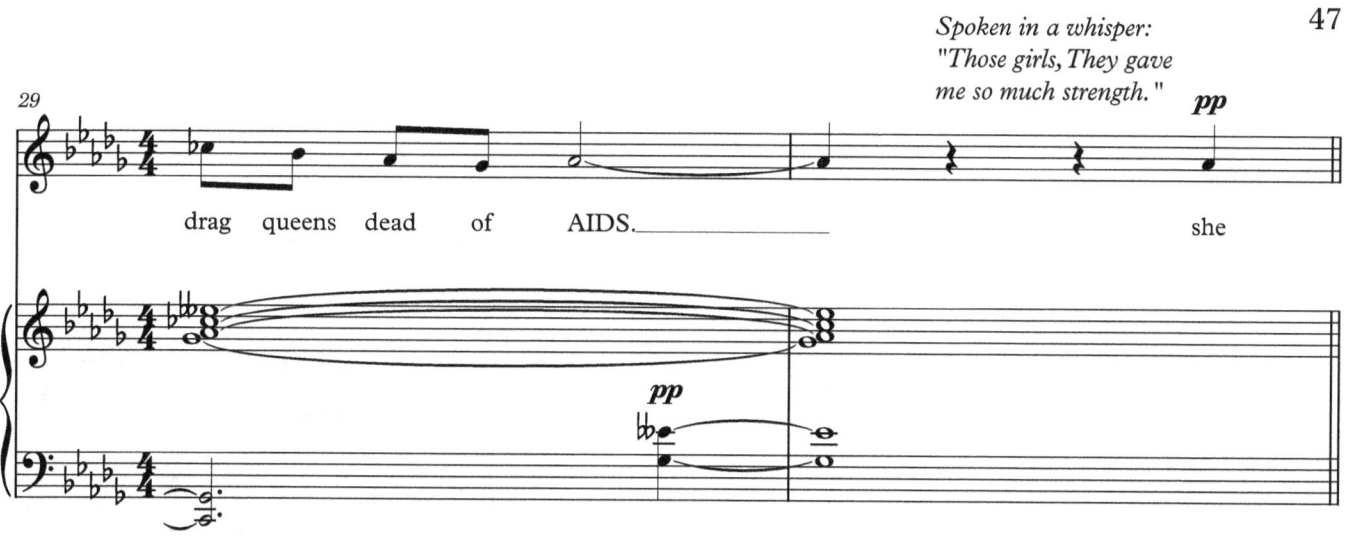

Princess Stories
from *Somewhere, Love*

JOEL E. JACOBSON

GARRETT HOPE
(2009)

© 2009, Garrett Evan Hope, Frog Princess Publishing. ASCAP. All Rights Reserved.
Text © 2008, J.E. Jacobson. All Rights Reserved.
Text used with permission of the author.

Like the Dove
from *Nostalgia*

ELI CARVAJAL

RORY WAINWRIGHT JOHNSTON
(2014)

Copyright © 2014 by Rory Wainwright Johnston. All Rights Reserved.
Text copyright © by Eli Carvajal. Used with permission.

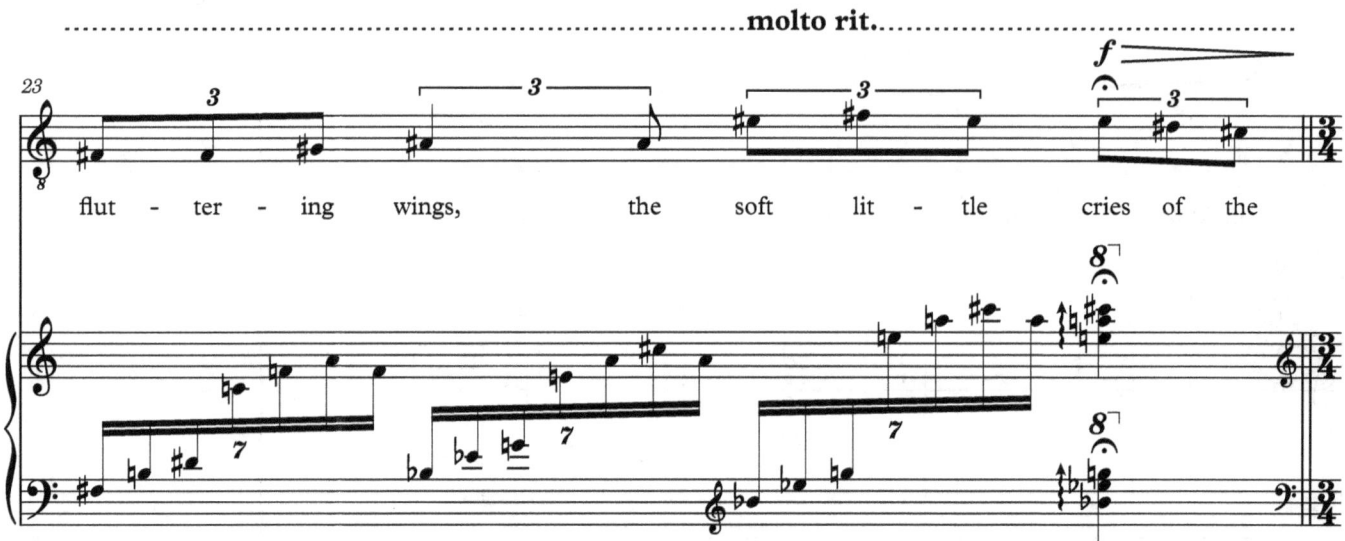
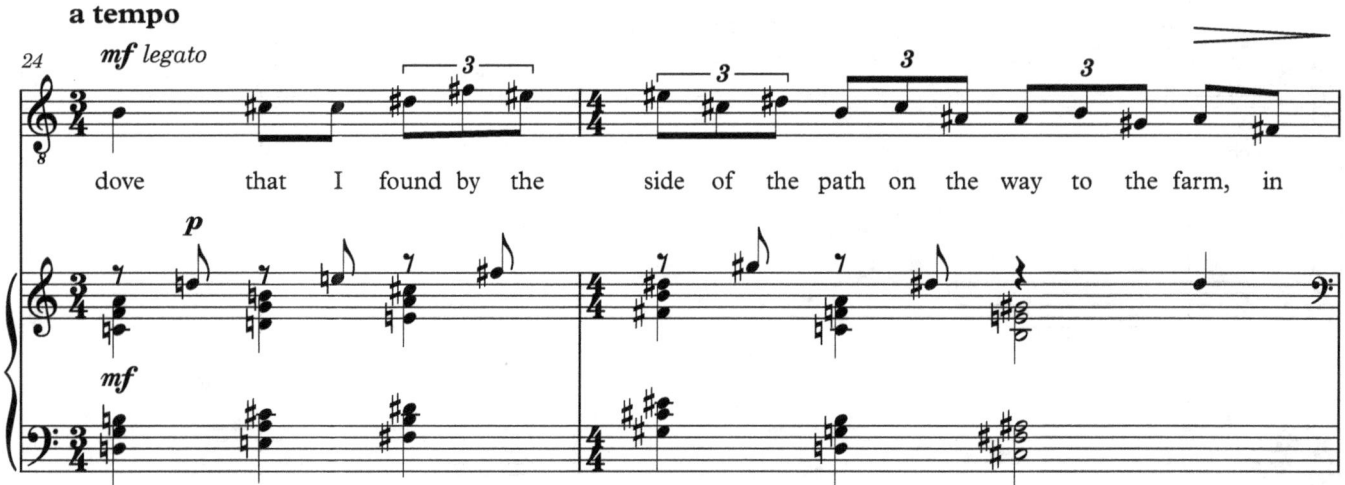

Love and Friendship
from *Confiding*

EMILY BRONTË
DAVID LEISNER

Copyright © 2010 by Merion Music, Inc. All Rights Reserved.
International Copyright Secured.

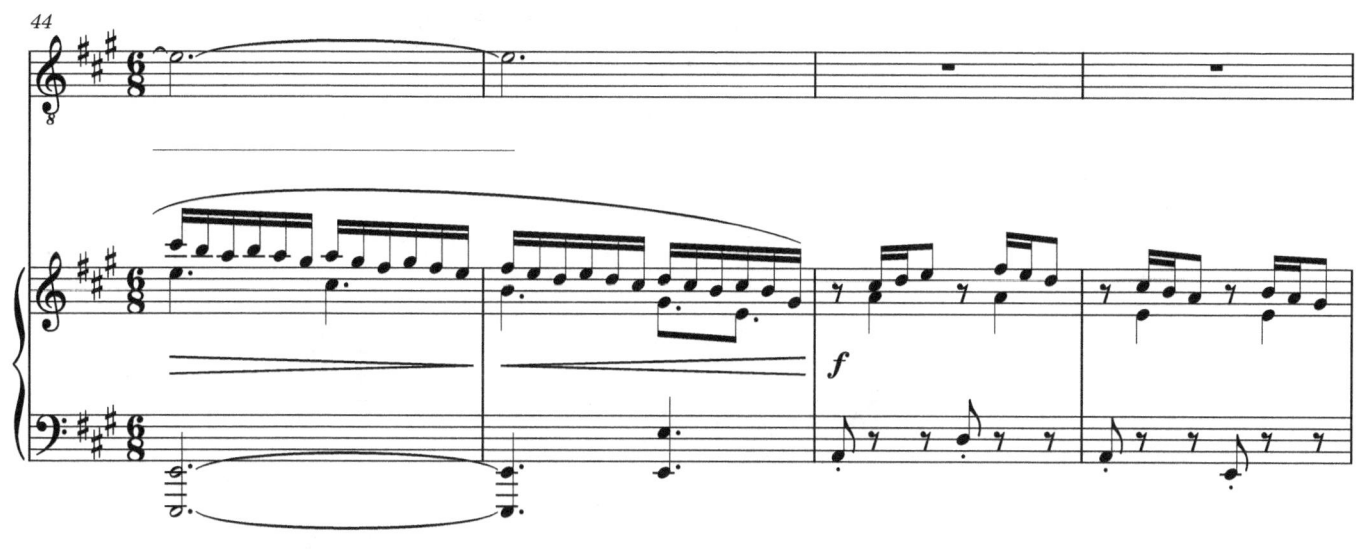

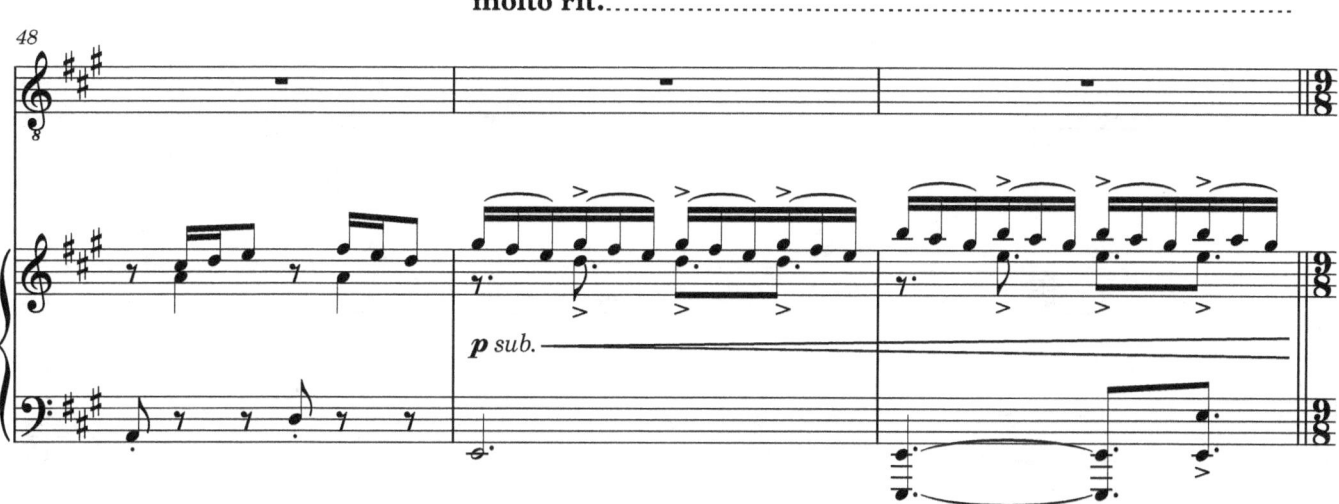

for James W. Harvey

Tuesdays and Thursdays

from *Snapshots*

ANONYMOUS

LISA NEHER
(2010)

With motion ♩ = 63

The best part of my Tues-days and Thurs-days

Copyright © 2010 by Lisa Neher (ASCAP), D.C. al Platypus Publishing Company.
Composer must be informed of all performances at: lisanehermusic@gmail.com.

Prick'd
from *Q or Eternity Promised*

WILLIAM SHAKESPEARE

FRANK J. OTERI
(2016)

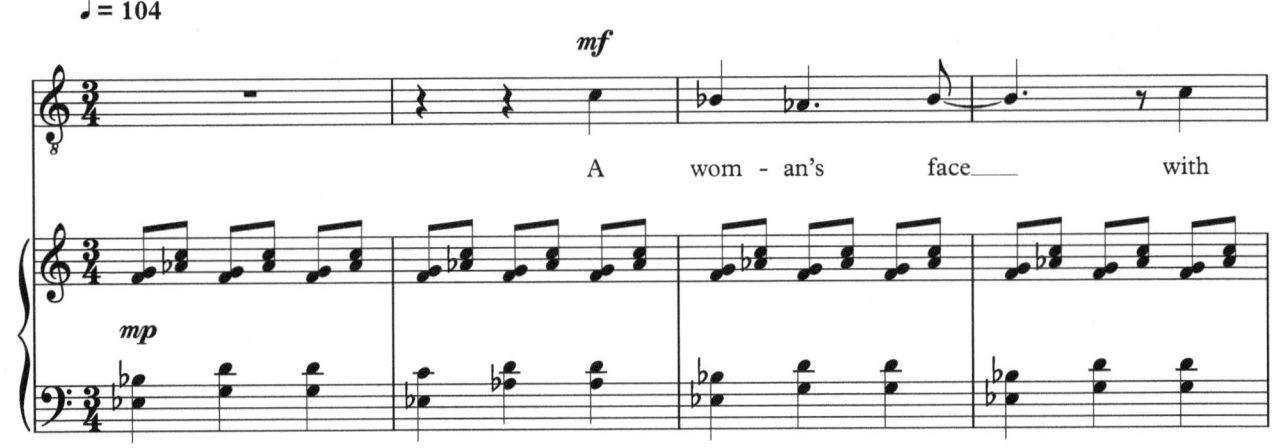

From *Q or Eternity Promised*: text by William Shakespeare (1564-1616), Public Domain.
Music (C) 2016 by Frank J. Oteri, Transformal Music (ASCAP).
All rights reserved. International Copyright Secured.

Black is the Color of My True Love's Hair
from *Three Folk Songs*

TRADITIONAL
Tempo I: Adagio, tenderly

GABRIELLE ROSSE OWENS
(2016)

* The word "black" is to be sung with sacred tones: shadow vowels Buh-Lah-Kuh. Black is more than just a color; c.f. Shakespeare's Dark Lady sonnet 130, "My mistress's eyes are nothing like the sun...if hairs be wires, black wires grow on her head..." Black is the color of secrets shouted from the mountaintop and a woman who has the power to break you with a look (see Sonnet 139).

Copyright © 2016 by Gabrielle Owens Music (ASCAP). All Rights Reserved.

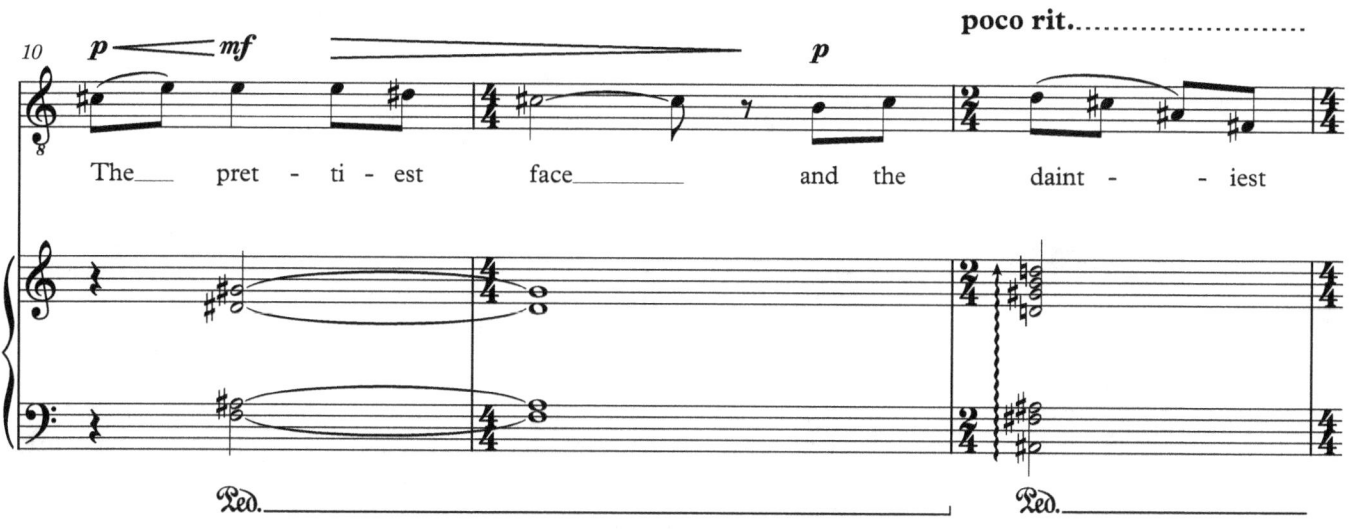

72

*Troublesome is a place: a lonely mountain

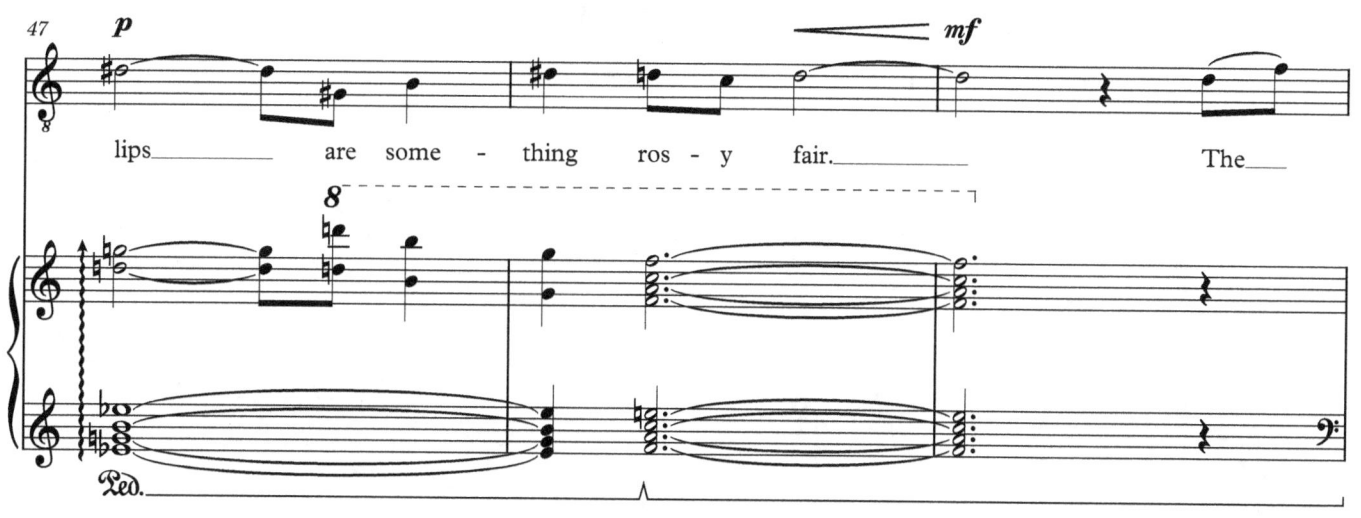

If Thou'lt Be Mine

from *Three Poems of Thomas Moore*

THOMAS MOORE

DARIEN SHULMAN
(2007)

Lyrics:

If thou'lt be mine, the treas-ures of air, Of earth, and sea, shall lie at thy feet;

Copyright © 2007 by Darien Shulman. All Rights Reserved.

to Marc Peloquin

John Anderson, My Jo
from *And He'll Be Mine*

ROBERT BURNS

DENNIS TOBENSKI
(2005)

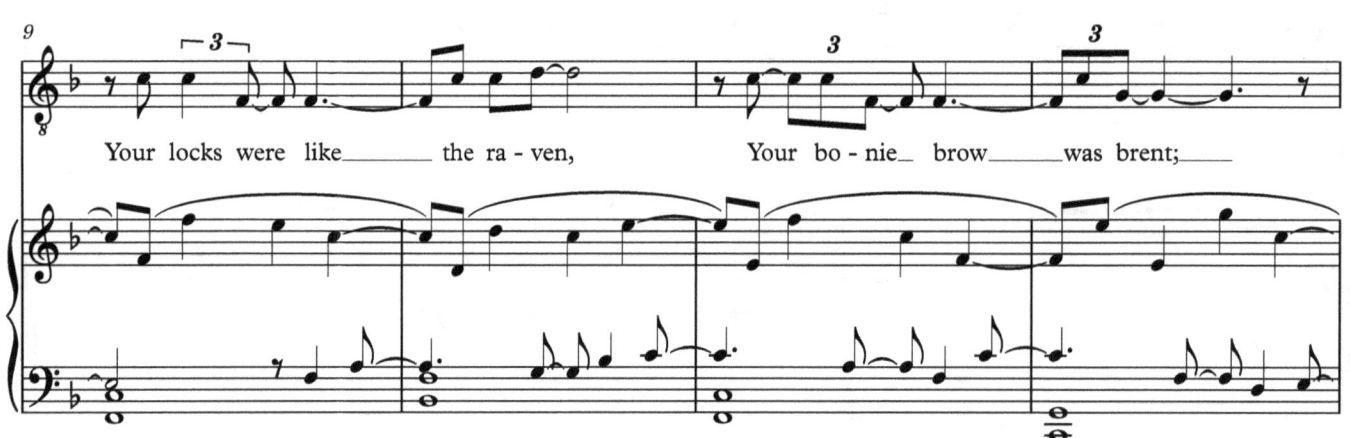

Copyright © 2005 by Dennis Tobenski. All Rights Reserved.

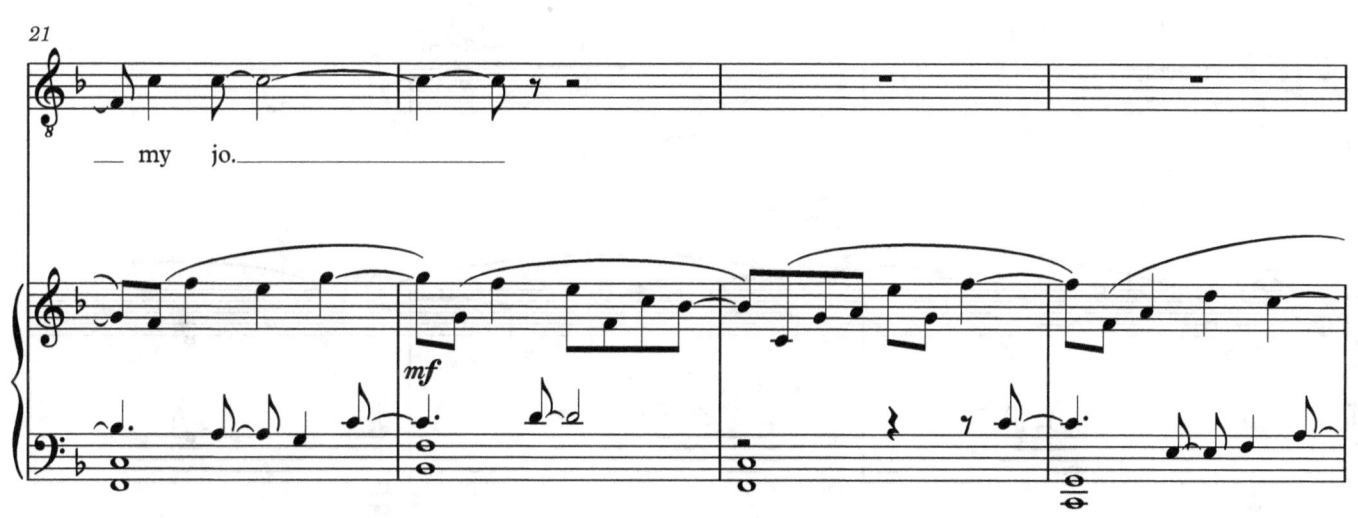

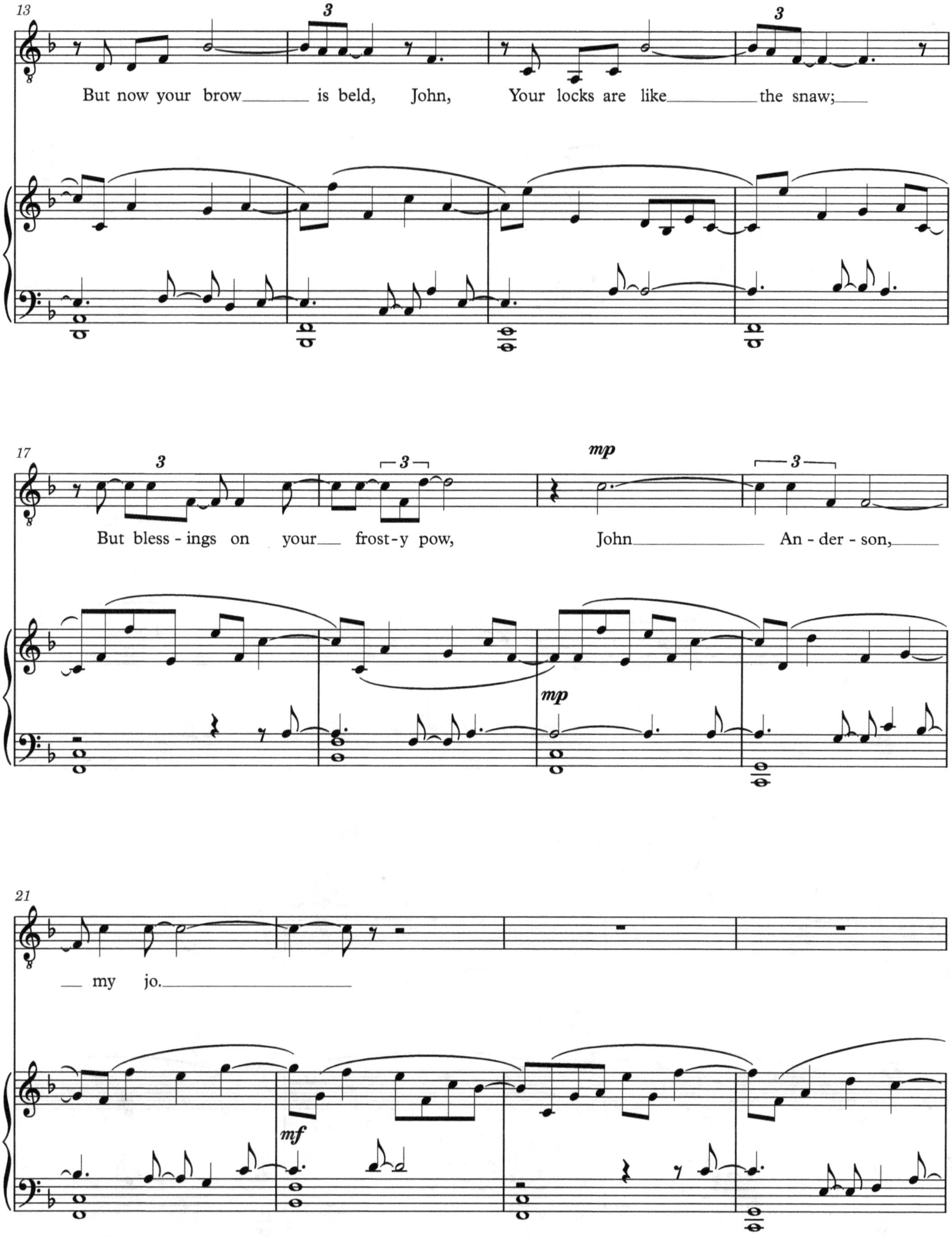
13
But now your brow is beld, John, Your locks are like the snaw;
17
But bless - ings on your frost - y pow, John An - der - son,
mp
mp
21
my jo.
mf

Here The Frailest Leaves Of Me
from *Leaves*

WALT WHITMAN

CRAIG URQUHART
(1980)

Let Me Play the Fool
from *Fools*

WILLIAM SHAKESPEARE
The Merchant of Venice, I.i

PHILIP WHARTON

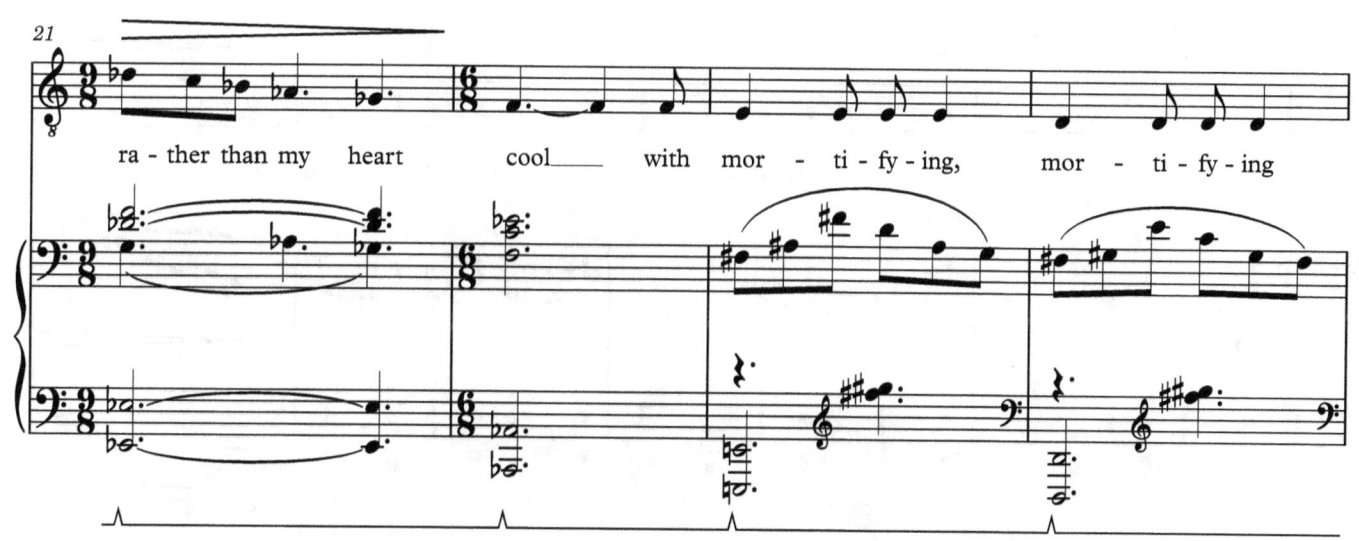

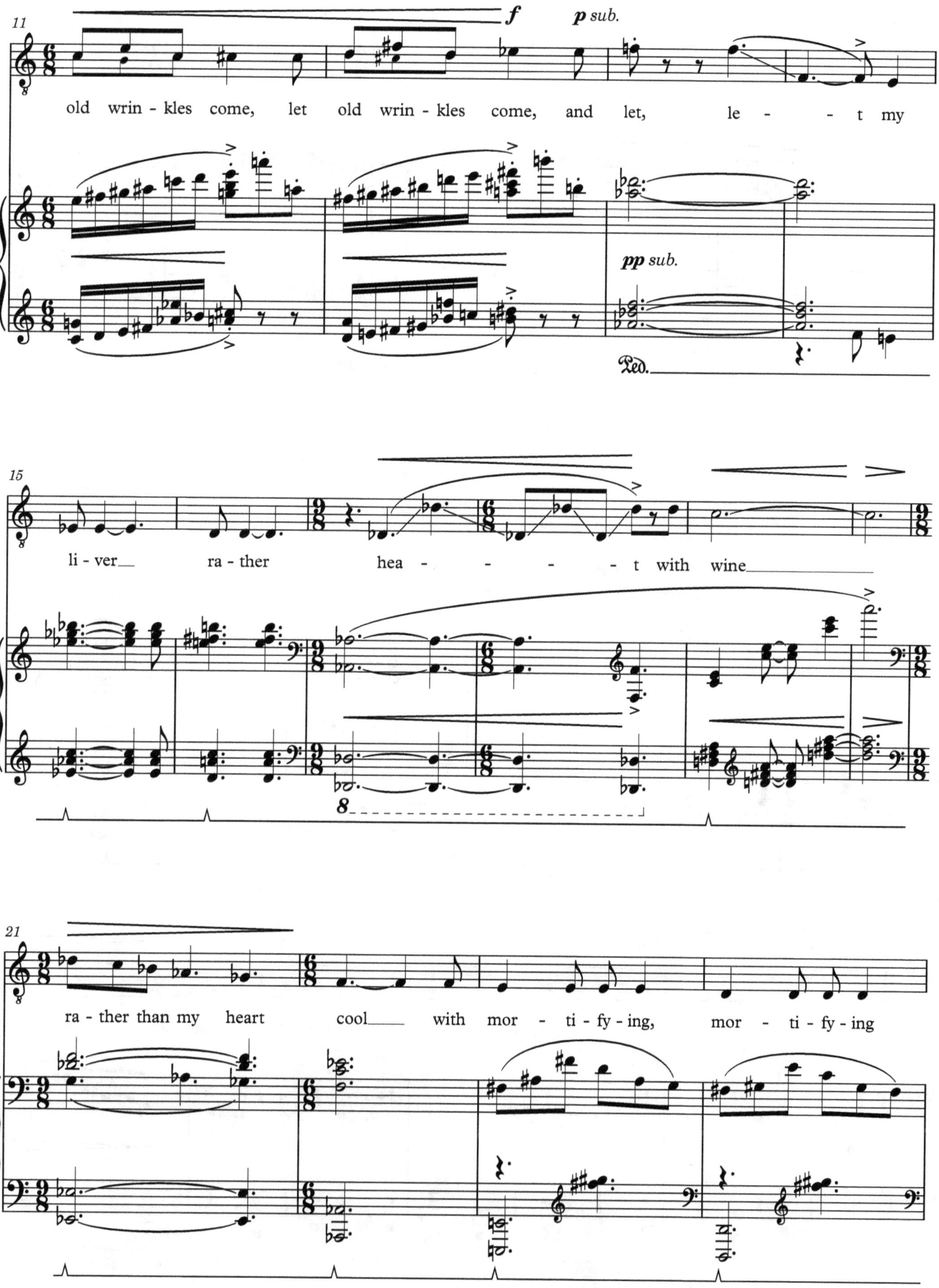
11
f
p sub.
old wrin - kles come, let old wrin - kles come, and let, le - - t my
pp sub.
Ped.
15
li - ver rather hea - - - t with wine
8
21
ra - ther than my heart cool with mor - ti - fy - ing, mor - ti - fy - ing

* *immediately close the vowel and sustain the pitch with the underlined consonants*

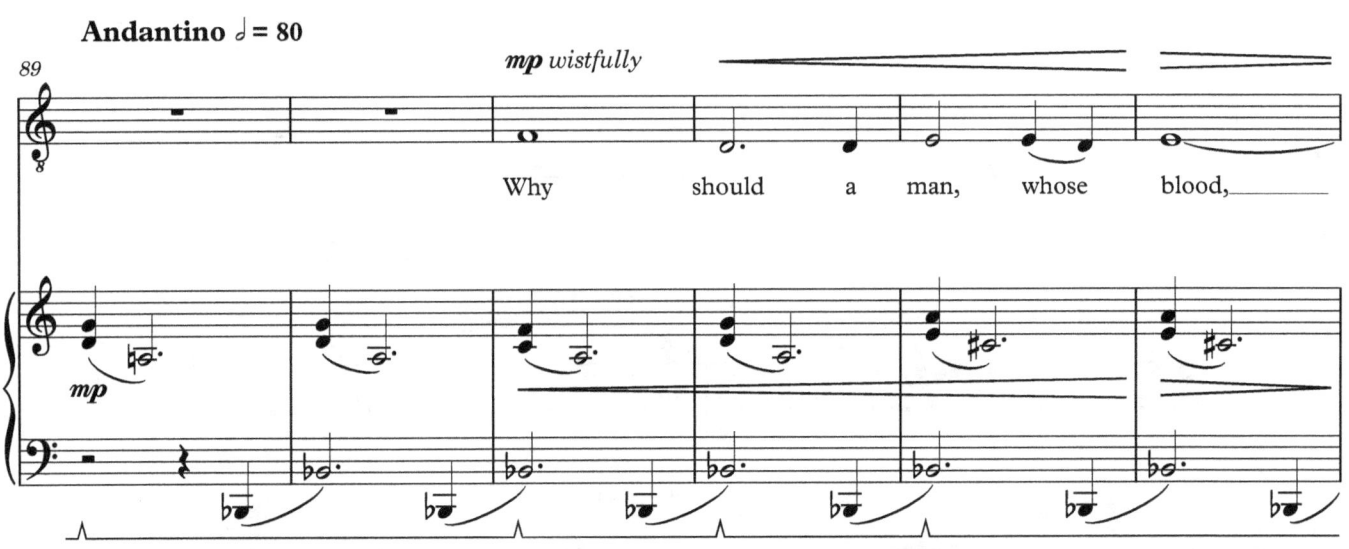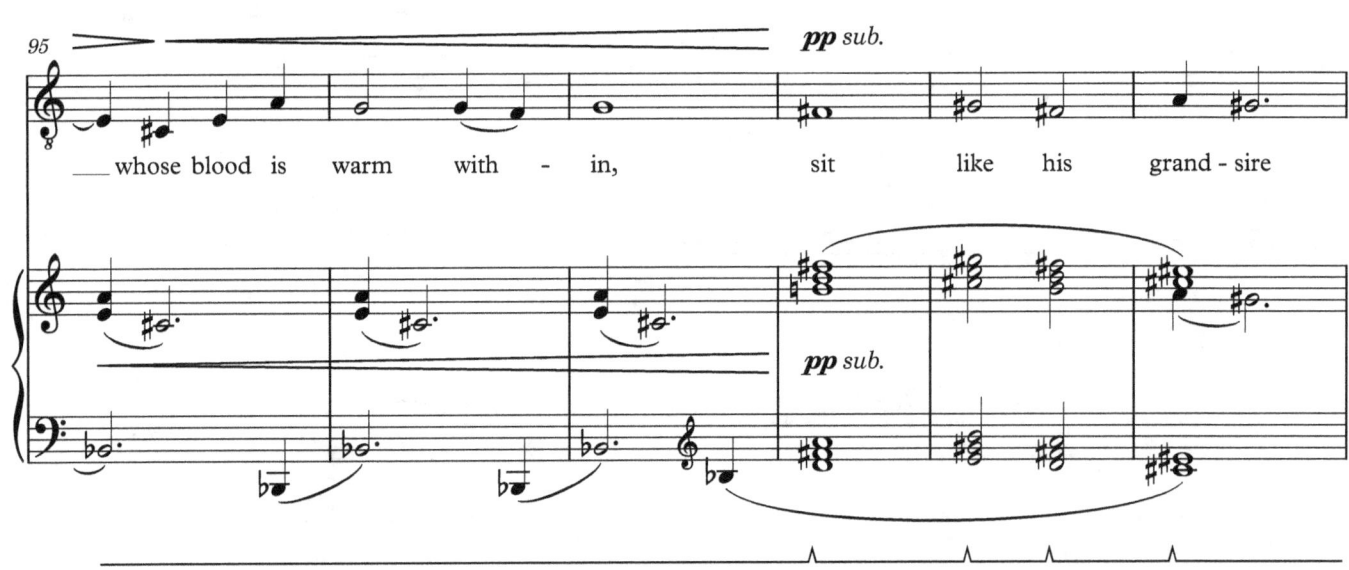

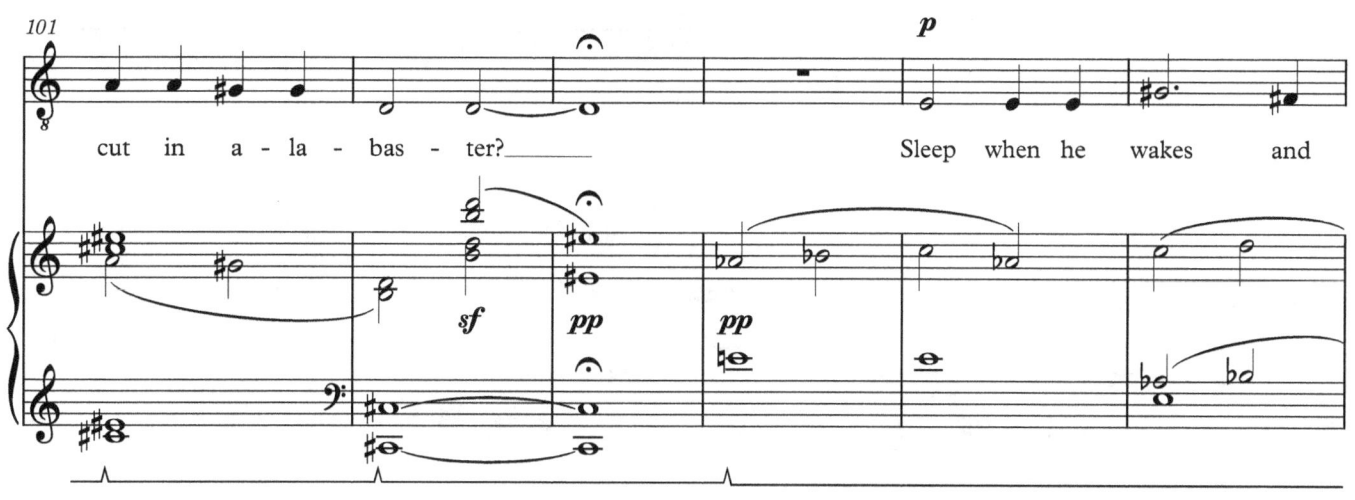
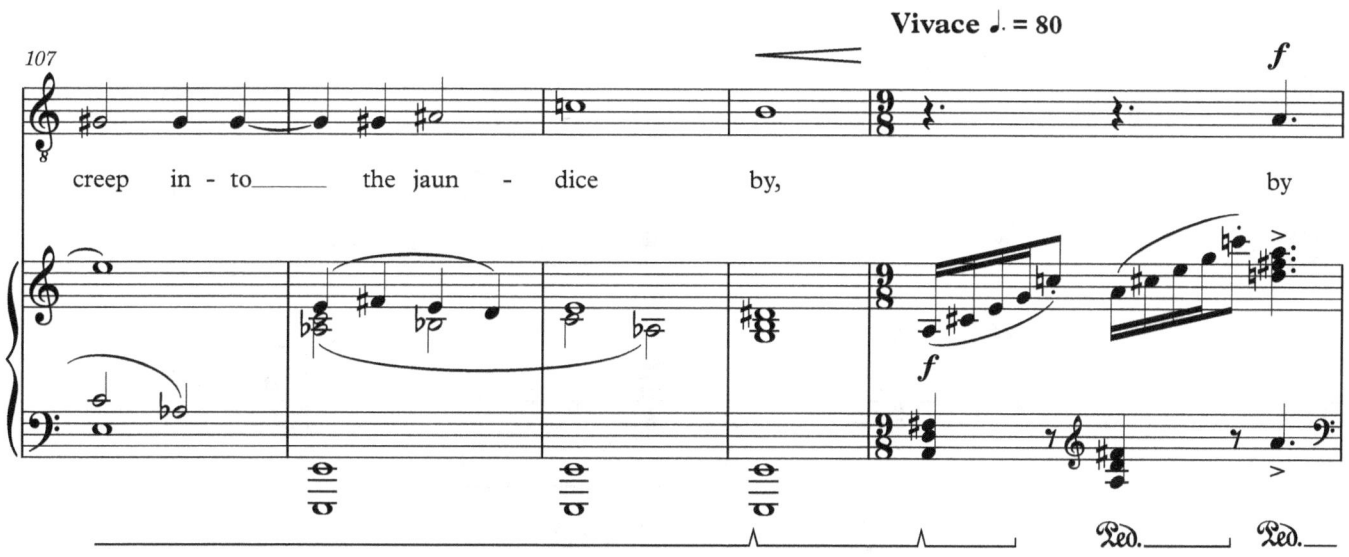

100

Commissioned by the Marilyn Horne Foundation and the ASCAP Foundation/Charles Kingsford Fund
for Dimitri Pittas

Night

from *Heaven and Earth*

WILLIAM BLAKE

SCOTT WHEELER
(2007)

Copyright © 2007 Scott Wheeler Music. All Rights Reserved.

102

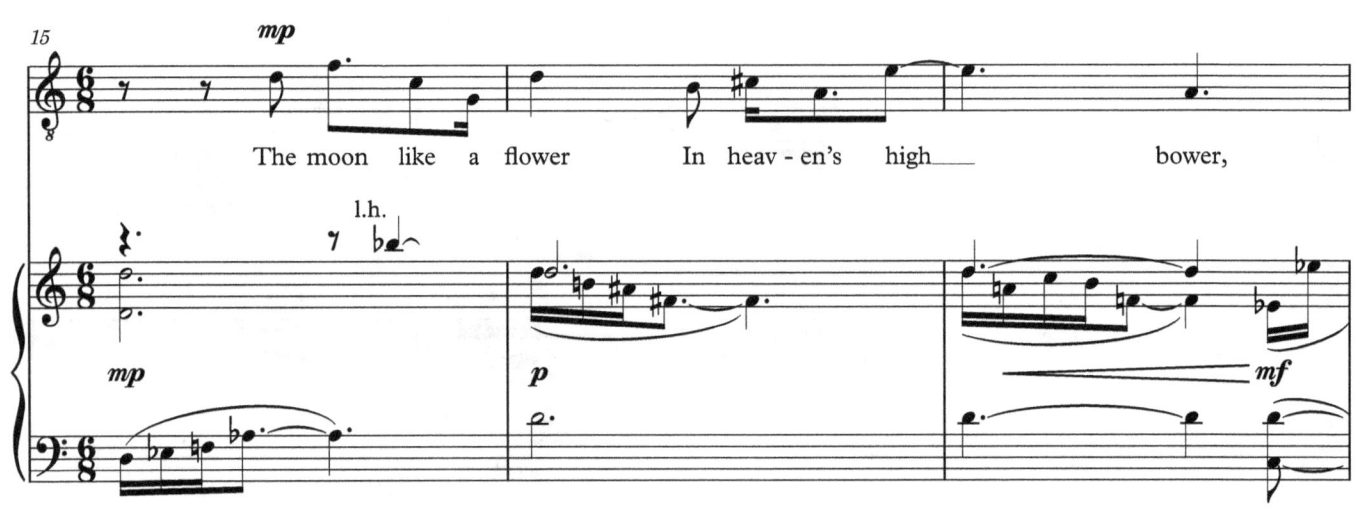

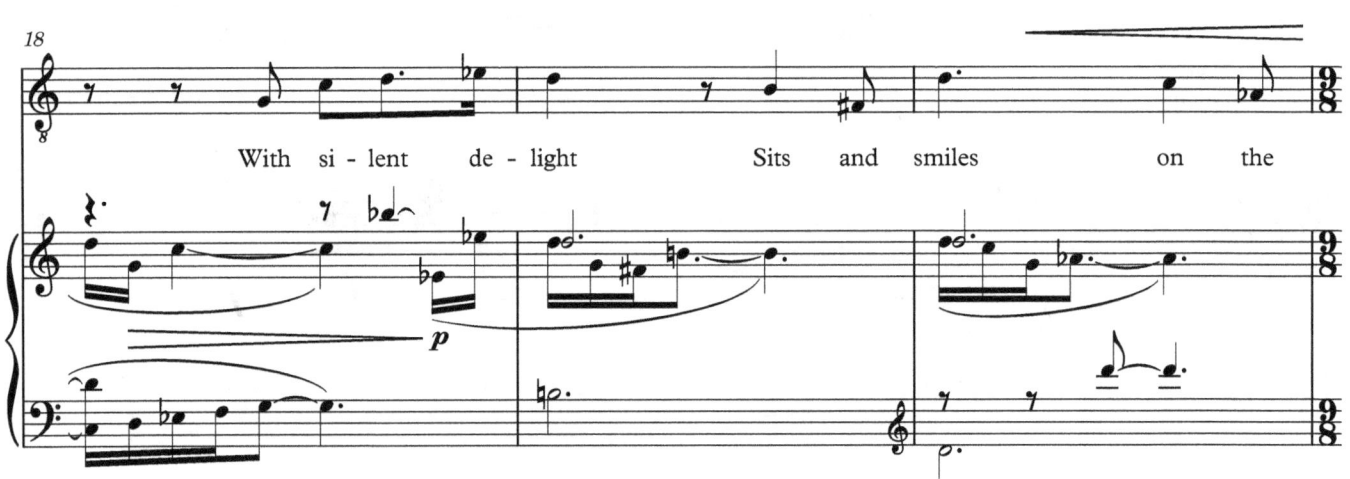

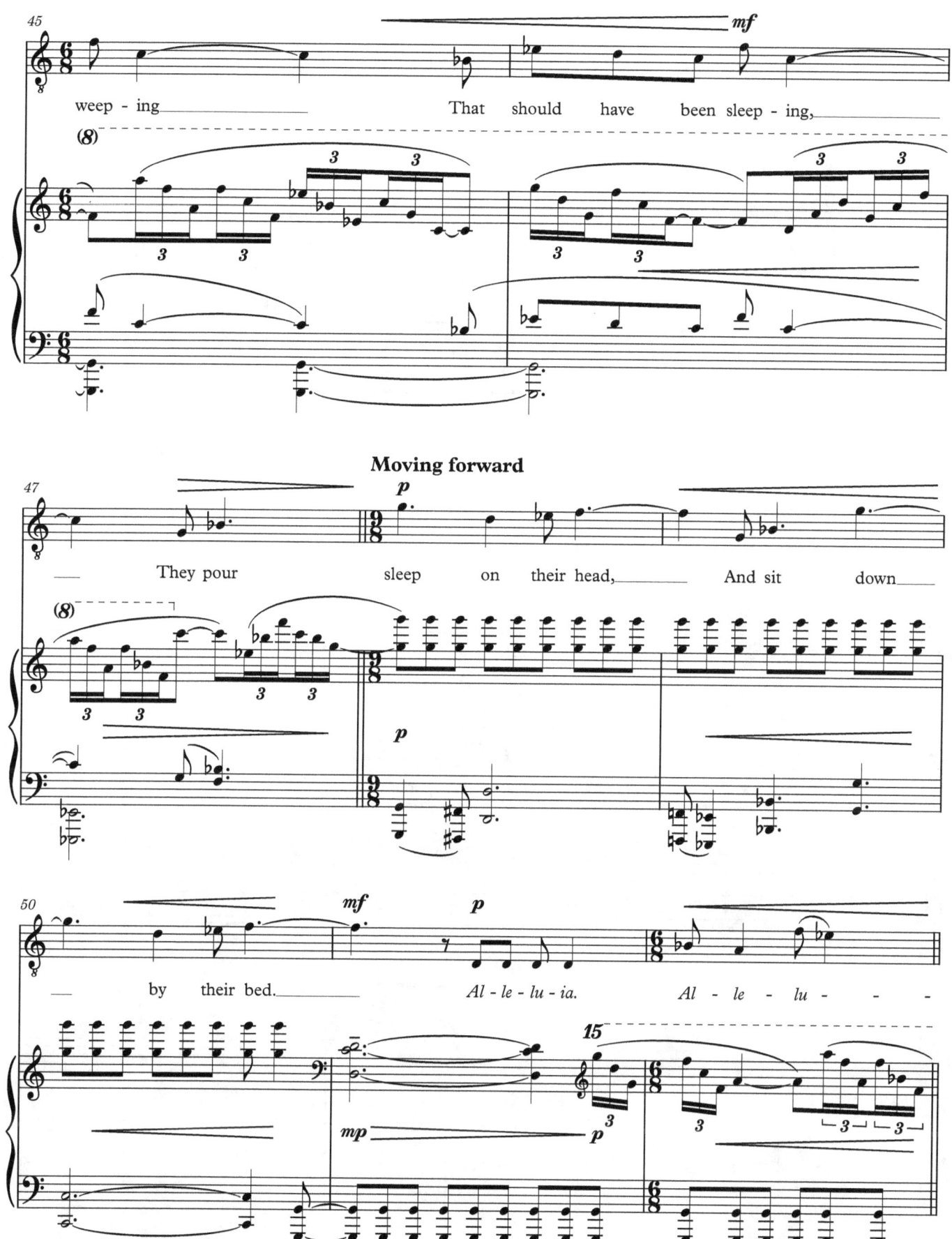

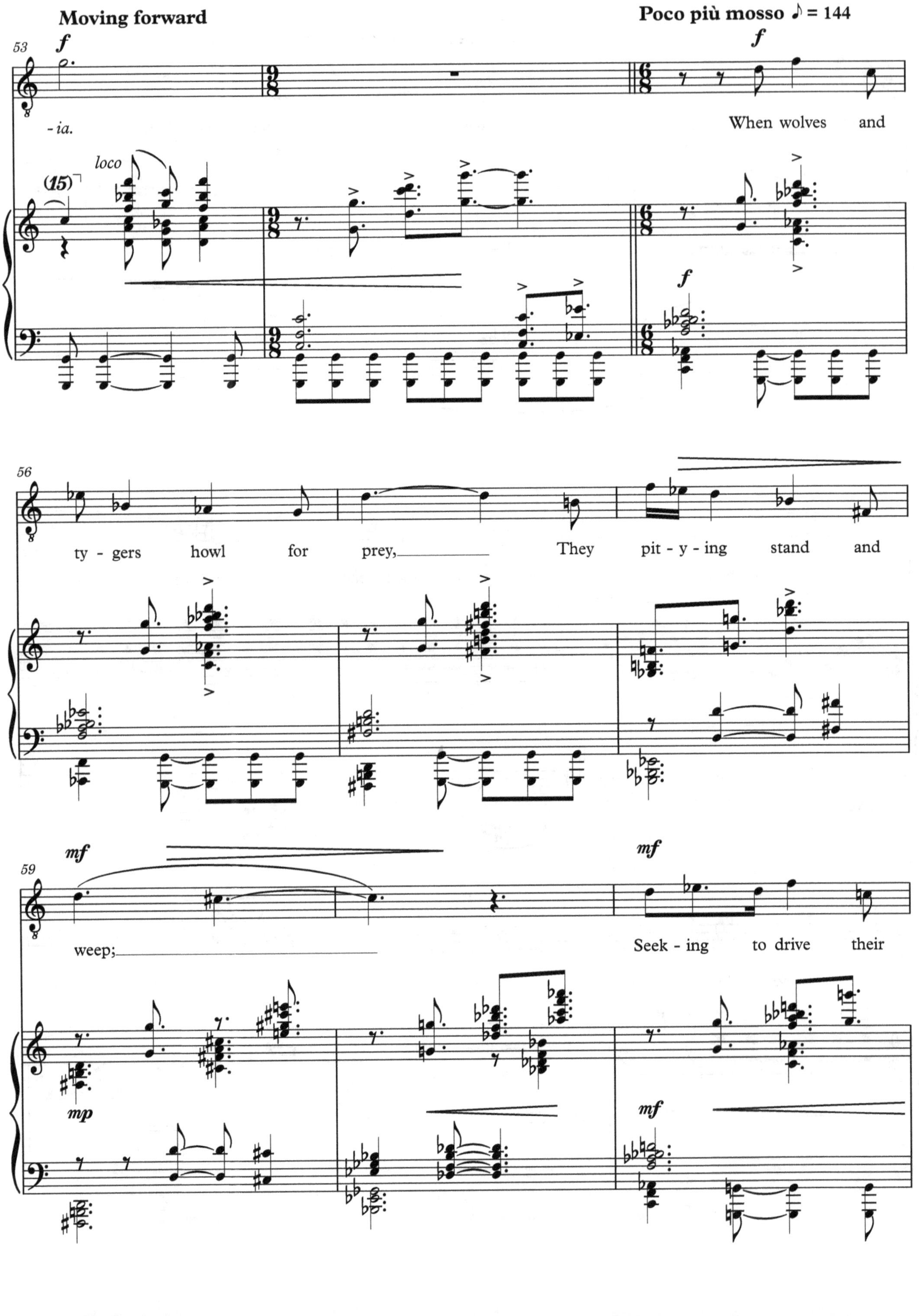
Moving forward
Poco più mosso ♪ = 144
f
-ia.
loco
(15)
f
When wolves and
f
ty - gers howl for prey,
They pit - y - ing stand and
mf
weep;
mp
mf
Seek - ing to drive their
mf

When First I Loved You

from *Six Love Songs*

Words and Music:
DAVID WOLFSON
(1998)

Copyright © 1999 by Wiwo Music. All Rights Reserved.

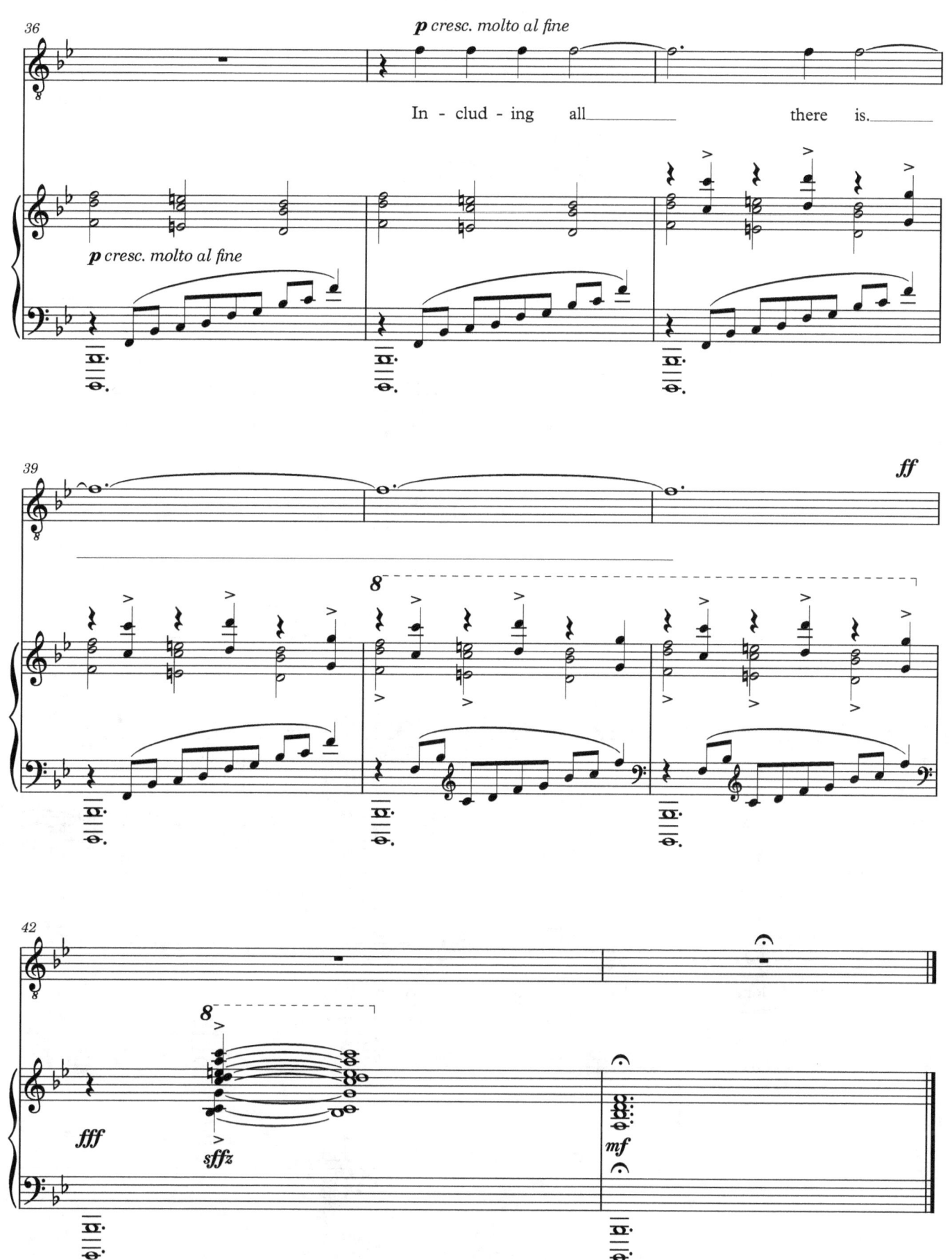

for Dennis Schebetta
River

Words and Music:
ROGER ZAHAB
(2016)

Words and music copyright © 2016 by Roger Zahab (BMI). All rights reserved.

118

About the Curator
Dennis Tobenski

dennis@dennistobenski.com
www.dennistobenski.com

Dennis Tobenski is a vocalist with a passion for performing new music by living composers. He is also a composer, and a strong advocate for new music and for the interests of living composers.

Called a "dynamic vocalist" by Anthony Tommasini of *The New York Times*, and "a skillful and sensitive singer who shapes phrases and renders text with expert care" by Gregory Berg of *Journal of Singing*, Dennis's focus as a vocalist is primarily on the works of the 21st and late 20th centuries. He has premiered works by David Del Tredici, Chester Biscardi, Ricky Ian Gordon, Darien Shulman, and Hadar Noiberg, among others.

In February 2016, he and pianist Marc Peloquin released their first album together, a disc of 19 art songs by living American composers titled *And He'll Be Mine*, which features works by David Del Tredici, Chester Biscardi, Zachary Wadsworth, Darien Shulman, and Dennis Tobenski.

Dennis hosts the *Music Publishing Podcast*, a music business-centered podcast aimed at helping composers and performers to learn more about the practical aspects of their careers.

He is also the founder of NewMusicShelf, a digital marketplace devoted to bringing together performers of new music and independently-published composers by offering a platform for composers to sell digital editions of their works.

Dennis received his B.Mus. in Vocal Performance and Music Theory & Composition from Illinois State University, and his M.A. in Music Composition from The City College of New York. He studied voice with baritone John M. Koch, and his principal composition teachers have included David Del Tredici, Chester Biscardi, and David Feurzeig. He is a member of the Board of Advisors for Composers Now, and the Board of Directors of the KeyedUp MusicProject.

Dennis lives in New York City with his husband Darien Scott Shulman and their cat Pistachio.

About the Composers

Paul Ayres

b. 1970

paulayres@clara.net
www.paulayres.co.uk

Paul Ayres was born in London (UK), studied music at Oxford University, and now works freelance as a composer & arranger, choral conductor & musical director, and organist & accompanist. He has received over one hundred commissions, and his works have been awarded or shortlisted for composition prizes in Bulgaria, Canada, Croatia, New Zealand, Poland, Russia, Spain, Switzerland, the UK and the USA. Paul particularly enjoys "re-composing" classical works (Purcell, Bach, Handel, Fauré) and "classicizing" pop music (jazz and show tunes, The Beatles, Happy Hardcore).

Most of Paul's compositions involve words, in pieces for solo voice, for choir, and for theatre. He collaborates with several poets, lyricists and librettists, and has set existing texts in Aramaic, ancient Greek, and West Yorkshire dialect. Stage works include the children's opera *The Stolen Moon*, the family opera *Just So: Tegumai's Tales*, and the two-hander *For Sale* (whose entire libretto is "For Sale. Baby Shoes. Never Worn.")

Of his solo CD *Handel-Inspired* (Priory), *The Gramophone* wrote: "Ayres is outstanding as composer, arranger, editor and skilful player... this CD is undoubtedly one of the most enjoyable and original recordings I've heard."

Paul is the regular conductor of City Chorus and the London College of Music Chorus (at the University of West London), accompanist of Concordia Voices, and associate accompanist of Crouch End Festival Chorus. He has led many music education workshops for children, and played piano for improvised comedy shows and musical theatre. Please visit www.paulayres.co.uk to find out more.

Chester Biscardi (BMI)

b. 1948

biscardi@slc.edu
www.chesterbiscardi.com

Chester Biscardi's music has been performed throughout Asia, Europe, and North and South America. His catalog includes *At the Still Point*, for orchestra, *Piano Concerto*, *Sailors & Dreamers*, for voice and chamber ensemble, the opera *Tight-Rope*, *Trasumanar* for twelve percussionists and piano, and works for piano, voice, chorus, and chamber ensembles, as well as incidental music for theatre, dance, and television. His work is published by C. F. Peters, Theodore Presser Company, and Biscardi Music Press. He is a recipient of the Rome Prize, a Guggenheim Fellowship, an Academy Award in Music from the American Academy and Institute of Arts and Letters, and a commission from the Koussevitzky Music Foundation in the Library of Congress, among numerous other awards and fellowships.

Born in Kenosha, Wisconsin in 1948, Biscardi studied English literature, Italian literature, and music composition at the University of Wisconsin-Madison before receiving a Doctor of Musical Arts degree from the Yale School of Music. His principal composition teachers included Kryszstof Penderecki, Toru Takemitsu, Les Thimmig, and Yehudi Wyner. He has been a member of the Music Faculty at Sarah Lawrence College since 1977.

Since the 1970s, Biscardi has been interested in the ways literature influences musical idea and form. Often a single word or poetic phrase generates the central idea of a composition, although his works are seldom overtly programmatic. The Italian *tenzone* [dialogue] inspired *Tenzone*, for two flutes and piano (1975), while T.S. Eliot's "Burnt Norton," with its interplay of form and time, evoked *At the Still Point* (1977). Timbral and spatial concerns also play an important role in his early works. Transparent textures, delicate nuances, and sounds frozen in space resonate from his study of Japanese music. In the 1985 opera, *Tight-Rope*, and the song cycle, *The Gift of Life* (1990–93), Biscardi's lyrical impulses, pervasive in his later works, are more pronounced. *Resisting Stillness* (1996), an intimate, strikingly spare work for two guitars, has autobiographical aspects, which are also a characteristic element of his mature music. His *Piano Quintet* (2004), written in memory of his father, uses elements from *The Odyssey* and several of his own earlier works, all of which, in the composer's words, "explore the passage of time, loss, recovery, and transcendence."

Clint Borzoni (ASCAP)

b. 1981

clintborzoni@gmail.com
www.clintborzoni.com

Clint Borzoni is an award-winning composer whose "highly original yet lyrical music…[and] natural gift for melody and harmonic structure" (*The Huffington Post*) has resulted in international performances and premieres.

His first opera with John de los Santos, *When Adonis Calls*, was premiered by Ashville Lyric Opera in May 2018, and will receive a second production by Thompson Street Opera and the Chicago Pride Center in September 2018. The full-length piece has also been presented by Fort Worth Opera, the Merola Opera Program, Opera America's New Works Forum, and operamission. Their second opera, *The Copper Queen*, won the top prize for Arizona Opera's commission program, Arizona SPARK, and is currently being developed by Arizona Opera. Borzoni's other operatic works have been performed by La MaMA, Symphony Space, the Glimmerglass Festival, the American Lyric Theater, the American Opera Projects, Opera on Tap, the Morgan Library & Museum, St Martin-in-the-Fields, and the Guildhall School of Music.

Mr. Borzoni has composed songs and song cycles for many leading vocalists. He won BARIHUNKS Best New Song (2015) and Best New Solo Work for Baritone (2017). He was also a winner of Sparks & Wiry Cries Second annual NYC songSLAM, and operamission's cabaret song competition.

Mr. Borzoni is the current Composer-in-Residence for Musica Marin, a nonprofit organization that presents, supports and inspires classical music throughout the San Francisco Bay Area. He studied with Pulitzer Prize-winning composer David Del Tredici at the City University of New York where he received an MA in Music Composition. He lives and works as a composer and teacher in NYC.

Facebook: www.facebook.com/clintborzonicomposer/
Twitter: @clintborzoni

Steven Burke (ASCAP)

b. 1967

steven.m.burke@gmail.com
www.stevenburkecomposer.com

Cited by the American Academy of Arts and Letters as a composer who "has that rarest of inventive gifts, a personal voice," Steven Burke is being recognized as one of the leading voices of his generation. His music has won praise for its emotional power and mastery. Mark Swed of the *Los Angeles Times* wrote "the writing has power…stinging emotions." Paul Griffiths of *The New York Times* wrote, his work "might have been written by Brahms after hearing the *Rite of Spring*… highly accomplished…bursting with historical awareness and creative confidence." A second citation from the American Academy of Arts and Letters reads: "It's rare, though, to hear music so distinctive, passionate, and compelling that suggests its composer is a voice for his generation. Steven Burke is one such fellow." Composer David Del Tredici, recognized as the father of the Neo-Romantic movement, has said on public radio: "There are some wonderful composers who are emerging now and who will be voices of their generation. One is Steven Burke, a remarkable composer. Completely trusting of his instinct, who writes passionate, wild, and completely controlled music."

Mr. Burke's distinctive work has been acknowledged by critics and singled out by several distinguished prizes and commissions including the Rome Prize and a Guggenheim Fellowship. He was awarded the Charles Ives Fellowship, as well as the Arts and Letters Award from the American Academy of Arts and Letters. He has received multiple fellowships from Yaddo, the MacDowell Colony, the Medway Institute, and an award from Meet the Composer. He was the first recipient of the Robbins Prize, and the White Flowers residency from Yaddo. He has received commissions from the Fromm Music Foundation at Harvard University, the Jerome Foundation, the National Symphony Orchestra, the St. Luke's Chamber Ensemble, Sequitur, the Raschèr Saxophone Quartet and the Albany Symphony. He has also been commissioned by Yaddo and the Orpheus Chamber Orchestra to compose a work commemorating the centennial of Yaddo. He was also commissioned by the Raschèr Saxophone Quartet and the Philharmonisches Orchester Kiel (Germany). to compose *Echo of Halos*, which was premiered in Germany to critical and public acclaim.

Daniel Gilliam (ASCAP)

b. 1978

danielgilliam@gmail.com
www.fictivemusic.com

Daniel Gilliam (b. 1978) is a composer from & living in Louisville, Kentucky. He was a resident at Copland House in 2017. Gilliam has been commissioned & collaborated with Kentucky Shakespeare, Louisville Ballet, Kentucky Governor's School for the Arts, pianist Lara Downes, violinist Rob Simonds, LONGLEASH (a piano trio), Steven Paul Spears, Youth Performing Arts School Chamber Choir (Louisville), Kentucky Center Chamber Players, & Jason Weinberger/Waterloo-Cedar Falls Symphony. Gilliam is a founding member of A/Tonal. His album of art songs *The Call to Earth* is available on iTunes. You can also find his music on Spotify & Bandcamp.

Twitter: @danielgilliam

Juliana Hall (ASCAP)

b. 1958

JH@JulianaHall.com
www.julianahall.com

American art song composer Juliana Hall (b. 1958) is a prolific and highly-regarded composer of vocal music, whose songs have been described as "brilliant" (Washington Post), "beguiling" (Times of London), and "the most genuinely moving music of the afternoon" (Boston Globe). Hall has composed works for renowned countertenor Brian Asawa, acclaimed mezzo soprano Stephanie Blythe, and star soprano Dawn Upshaw, as well as for numerous organizations including Feminine Musique, Lynx Project, Lyric Fest, and the Seattle Art Song Society. Venues across America and worldwide including Carnegie Hall's Weill Recital Hall, the Library of Congress, Morgan Library & Museum, and Wigmore Hall, as well as the London Festival of American Music, Norfolk Chamber Music Festival, Ojai Music Festival, and Tanglewood Music Center have all hosted her work. St. Paul's Cathedral in London presented Hall's songs in a Holy Week meditation service in 2015, and the Joy in Singing organization in New York presented her songs on their "Edward T. Cone Composers Concert" at Lincoln Center in 2016. In 2017 Hall received SongFest's Sorel Commission, and in 2018 she was Guest Composer at the Fall Island Vocal Arts Seminar. Concerts devoted to Hall's music have also been presented by New York's Casement Fund Song Series in 2016, Princeton's Contemporary Undercurrent of Song Project in 2017, and London's "re-Sung" art song series in 2018. Hall is a Guggenheim Fellow (1989) with a Master's degree from Yale (1987), and her art songs are published by E. C. Schirmer and Boosey & Hawkes.

Drew Hemenger (BMI)

b. 1968

www.hemenger.com

Emerging as a composer with a unique, yet quintessentially American sound, Drew Hemenger's music has been heard all over North America, Europe, and as far as Russia and Asia. Described as "deceptively simple" (*NewMusicBox*); "perfectly crazy" (*Sequenza21*); and "unlike anything I've heard before - in a good way!" (Ned Rorem), Hemenger's music has been performed in venues ranging from Carnegie Hall and Lincoln Center to intimate churches in the Midwest. Although he now considers himself a New Yorker, Hemenger remains close to his Ohio roots.

His works have been commissioned by distinguished artists and institutions, both here and abroad. These include the *AIDS Quilt Songbook @ 20* (*Her Final Show*), The Auros Ensemble (*For Robin*), Chamber Music Yellow Springs (*Three Inner Moments: String Quartet No. 2*, for The Vogler Quartet), Sweden's Duo Con Forza (*Petit Duo*), the Goldman Memorial Band (*Manhattan Flourish*), Madrid's Jones & Maruri Cello/Guitar Duo (*Songs From America*), The Lively Arts at Indiana University of Pennsylvania (*An Evening in the Harlem Renaissance*), Chicago's Orion Ensemble (*Which Way Home?*), pianists Pascal and Ami Rogé (*Four Places in New York*, piano 4-hands version), Symphony New Hampshire (*Marifé Suite*), and the University of Texas at Austin (*Sharks*, for violinist Brian Lewis).

Commercial recordings include *Songs from America* performed by the Jones & Maruri Cello/Guitar Duo on EMEC Discos and *Her Final Show* performed by Anthony Dean Griffey and Thomas Bagwell on the new CD *An Aids Quilt Songbook: Sing for Hope* on GPR Records.

Hemenger earned a Bachelor's degree in Trumpet Performance from Ohio Wesleyan University, after which he studied composition at The Juilliard School with Stanley Wolfe. His Master's and Doctoral degrees are from the Manhattan School of Music where he studied principally with Richard Danielpour. Other teachers and mentors include George Crumb, David Del Tredici, Sebastian Currier, and Robert Beaser.

Garrett Hope (ASCAP)

b. 1978

www.garretthope.com

Garrett is a provider of experiences. He loves working with students and educators to help change the lives of young people through writing, commissioning, and performing freshly composed music. He's won a few awards and has a doctorate in composition. He also hosts *The Portfolio Composer* podcast.

    Facebook: www.facebook.com/garretthopecomposer
    Twitter: @ composergarrett

Rory Wainwright Johnston

b. 1993

www.soundcloud.com/rorywjohnstoncomposer

Rory is a conductor, composer, tenor and pianist from Bradford-on-Avon near Bath. Rory read Music at the University of Manchester, graduating in 2016 with a First Class degree. He is staying on at the University to work towards a MusM Masters degree in Instrumental Composition with Camden Reeves.

During his time at as an undergraduate, Rory was heavily involved with the Music Society, conducting both the choirs (University Chorus, Cosmo Singers and Ad Solem) and the orchestras (Symphony Orchestra, Chamber Orchestra, Wind Orchestra and the New Music Ensemble) for his second and third years, culminating in a performance of Arvo Pärt's Adam's Lament for Choir and String Orchestra. In his final year he was appointed the Musical Director of the University's Chamber Choir, Ad Solem, enjoying a successful year of concerts and recordings.

As a pianist and tenor, Rory has performed in many capacities. A treble in the Bath Abbey Choir from 2003-2008, his last two as Head Chorister, he re-joined the choir as a Tenor in 2011, going on to sing in live broadcasts on BBC Radio 3 and 4, as well as on the choirs CD recordings. Rory studied piano with internationally renowned harpsichordist Sophie Yates from 2003-2013, with whom he studied for his dipABRSM piano diploma. Under her tutelage Rory twice participated in piano masterclasses with Joanna MacGregor, one of which lead to a performance of Debussy on one of Rachmaninov's pianos held at the Holburne Museum in Bath. Whilst at University, Rory studied piano for two years with Richard Casey, before focussing on conducting under the mentorship of Justin Doyle and Mark Heron.

Currently, Rory is the Musical Director of Cantores Olicanae, The Brixi Singers, as well as continuing to support the University Music Society as a choral conductor whilst completing his Masters Degree. He is also the founder and Musical Director of the Manchester Renaissance Ensemble, a choir and pool of instrumentalists focussed on the performance of early music.

David Leisner (BMI)

b. 1953

leisnerdavid@gmail.com
www.davidleisner.com

David Leisner maintains a triple career as guitarist, composer and teacher. Vocal music has played a central role in his composition catalog, which otherwise includes orchestral and chamber works.

The Boston Globe's Richard Dyer wrote, "He shows imagination and taste in taking poems from disparate sources and putting them into cycles that trace emotional progress and develop dramatic shape. His prosody is excellent, and he sets words with an ear for sound, rhythm and sense…Best of all, Leisner has a gift for eloquently shaping a vocal line that is also grateful to sing." His catalog includes song sets and cycles for voice and piano - *Confiding, To Sleep, O Love is the Crooked Thing* – voice and guitar – *Confiding, Three James Tate Songs, Outdoor Shadows, West Wind, Simple Songs, Eve's Diary, Heaven's River, Five Songs of Devotion, Four Yiddish Songs - Fidelity* (tenor/soprano, baritone and piano), *Of Darkness and Light* (tenor, violin, oboe and piano), *A Timeless Procession* (baritone and string quartet), *Das Wunderbare Wesen* (baritone and cello).

His vocal music has been sung by such eminent artists as Sanford Sylvan, Wolfgang Holzmair, Kurt Ollmann, Michael Kelly, Thomas Meglioranza, Robert Osborne, Patrick Mason, Rufus Müller, William Ferguson, Paul Sperry, Andrew Fuchs, James Onstad, Dennis Tobenski, Carole Farley, Devony Smith, Juliana Gondek, Susan Narucki, Trudy Craney, D'Anna Fortunato, and Heather Johnson.

His works are published by Theodore Presser Co., G. Schirmer, Doberman-Yppan and Columbia Music. A graduate of Wesleyan University, he studied composition with Richard Winslow, Virgil Thomson, Charles Turner and David Del Tredici.

Lisa Neher (ASCAP)

b. 1985

lisanehermusic@gmail.com
www.lisanehermusic.com

Composer and Mezzo-Soprano Lisa Neher (b. 1985) writes theatrical, story-driven music for instruments and voices. Trained as a stage actress, her compositions are shaped by her keen sense of dramatic timing and feature aching, lyrical phrases, energetic rhythmic motives, and intense harmonies. Lisa's particular passion for text and poetry has led to works such as her chamber opera *White Horizon*, about a nineteenth-century Arctic expedition gone wrong. She often draws inspiration for her instrumental works from the natural world, suggesting the joyous bubbling of streams, the delicacy of sprouting plants, and the eerie mystery of deep ocean life with evocative timbres and vivid motives.

Lisa's commissions include works for Duward Ensemble, the Glass City Singers, Coe College Orchestra, Kirkwood Community College Chamber Singers, pianist Michael Kirkendoll, and flutist Rose Bishop. Her marimba duo *Thaw* was premiered by Mayumi Hama and Chris Froh at the Sacramento State Festival of New American Music. She is a fellow of the Cortona Sessions for New Music and the Gabriela Lena Frank Creative Academy of Music.

Lisa is in high demand as a performer of contemporary and standard repertoire and is the creator of the One Voice Project, a one-woman performance combining contemporary poetry and new musical works for unaccompanied voice chosen through a call for scores initiative. She spends her free time distance running, watching science fiction movies, and baking delicious treats involving copious amounts of chocolate. For more information, visit her website, www.lisanehermusic.com.

Twitter:	@LisaNeher
Instagram:	@lisanehermezzo
Soundcloud:	www.soundcloud.com/lisa-neher
Facebook:	@LisaNeherMusic
YouTube:	https://www.youtube.com/c/LisaNeher

Frank J. Oteri (ASCAP)

b. 1964

tc@blackteamusic.com
www.blackteamusic.com/artists/frank-j-oteri

Frank J. Oteri's voracious musical appetite finds many avenues of expression, but ultimately all lead back to his musical compositions which combine emotional directness with an obsession for formal processes. Oteri's syncretic compositional style has been described as "distinctive" in *The Grove Dictionary of American Music* and his music has been performed on five continents in venues ranging from Carnegie Hall's Weill Recital Hall in New York City, Conservatory Hall in St. Petersburg, Russia, and the Central Conservatory of Music in Beijing, China to Seattle's PONCHO Concert Hall and the Andy Warhol Museum in Pittsburgh. MACHUNAS, Oteri's performance oratorio created in collaboration with Italian visual artist Lucio Pozzi and inspired by the life of Fluxus-founder George Maciunas, premiered during the Christopher Festival in Vilnius, Lithuania in 2005. Interpreters of Oteri's music include pianist Sarah Cahill, harpsichordist Rebecca Pechefsky, clarinetist Michiyo Suzuki, guitarists Dominic Frasca and David Starobin, the Ray-Kallay Duo, the Cheah Chan Duo, Duo Montagnard, Pentasonic Winds, Sylvan Winds, Magellan String Quartet, the PRISM Saxophone Quartet, the Los Angeles Electric 8, the Locrian Chamber Players, Central City Chorus, and the Young People's Chorus of New York City. In addition to his compositional activities, Oteri is the Composer Advocate at New Music USA and the Co-Editor of *NewMusicBox*, a web magazine he founded which has been online since May 1999. In 2007, he was the recipient of ASCAP's Victor Herbert Award and, in 2016, he was elected to the Executive Committee of the International Society for Contemporary Music (ISCM).

Gabrielle Rosse Owens (ASCAP)

b. 1982

owens.gabrielle@gmail.com
www.soundcloud.com/gabrielle_owens

Gabrielle Rosse Owens is an award-winning composer of music for orchestra, chorus and chamber ensemble. Orchestral works include *When Evening Comes* (2017) and *Royal Diadem* (2017), recorded with the UCLA Philharmonia in 2018. Recent chamber works include *The Tell-Tale Heart* (2018), written for the Moscow Contemporary Music Ensemble; *Homeward Flight* (2018), written for Armen Ksajikian, associate principal cellist with the Los Angeles Chamber Orchestra; *Balancing Act*, performed by pianist José Menor; and *Three Folk Songs* (2016), winner of the Boston New Music Initiative's 2017 Call for Scores. Upcoming projects include *The Prophecy of Daniel* (2018), a one act monodrama in three scenes with soprano Hila Plitmann and the Lyris Quartet. Honors and awards include the Elaine Krown Klein Award, the Deglin Award, President's Scholar, Phi Beta Kappa, and full scholarships to the Sorbonne University, Temple University and UCLA. She is currently pursuing doctoral studies in composition at UCLA.

Darien Scott Shulman (ASCAP)

b. 1980

darien@darienshulman.com
www.darienshulman.com

Darien Shulman is a composer of music for film and television.

He frequently collaborates with up-and-coming directors and producers – most notably, the creative team behind Woodhead Entertainment, with whom he worked to score the Netflix original series, *American Vandal*, which entered its second season in September 2018. Working closely with Woodhead, Darien has provided the musical voice for the bulk of their digital shorts, many of which have amassed millions of views on YouTube, Vimeo, and Funny Or Die.

He also composes music for feature-length films, such as *Funeral Kings*, directed by the McManus Brothers, which was highlighted at the SXSW and Fantasia film festivals.

Through his long, collaborative relationship with Storefront Music, Darien has composed music for a number of high profile television commercials, including spots for Snickers (which premiered during the 2016 Superbowl), Verizon, American Express, Kleenex, Comcast, Citibank, and others. His music has also been featured in several segments of show TripTank on Comedy Central.

A graduate of Northwestern University and The Juilliard School, Darien remains active as a concert music composer, with performances and recordings by various ensembles in his birthplace of New York City, where he continues to live and work.

Dennis Tobenski (ASCAP)

b. 1982

dennis@dennistobenski.com
www.dennistobenski.com

Dennis Tobenski is a composer of acoustic new music, a vocalist, and a strong advocate for new music and the interests of living composers.

Dennis' *Only Air*, a 20-minute work for high voice and orchestra memorializing the gay teenagers who have taken their own lives in recent years, was commissioned by the Illinois State University Symphony Orchestra, and has been performed in a chamber version by The Secret Opera in New York and members of the Bay Area Rainbow Symphony in San Francisco.

The voice features prominently in his catalog of works, with a special emphasis on working with texts by living poets. He has collaborated with such poets as Jorn Ake, Idris Anderson, Kathryn Levy, Elizabeth Seydel Morgan, Maggie Smith, Mark Statman, and Patricia Valdata.

Dennis received his B.Mus. in Vocal Performance and Music Theory & Composition from Illinois State University, and his M.A. in Music Composition from The City College of New York.

His principal teachers have included David Del Tredici, Chester Biscardi, Serra Hwang, Stephen Andrew Taylor, and David Feurzeig. He is a member of the Board of Advisors for Composers Now, and the Board of Directors of Perfect Enemy Records and KeyedUp MusicProject.

Dennis lives in New York City with his husband Darien Scott Shulman and their cat Pistachio.

Facebook: www.facebook.com/dennistobenski
Twitter: @dennistobenski

Craig Urquhart (ASCAP)

b. 1953

www.craigurquhart.com

The music of composer/pianist Craig Urquhart is a continuing renewal of faith in beauty and the healing power of music.

Craig continues on his musical path with his latest CD release *Calm Seas*. *Calm Seas* is Craig's ninth solo piano album. His previous acclaimed albums are: *First Light, Within Memory, Secret Spaces, Streamwalker, Evocation, Songs Without Words, The Dream of the Ancient Ones*, and *Epitaphs and Portraits*.

Craig has performed throughout the United States, and has also toured in Japan, Italy, Germany, France and Belgium. Craig continues to share his music in new and various ways. He supplied many solo piano works for the soundtrack to the 2010 Teddy Award Winning (Berlinale) film *Postcards To Daddy*.

Craig contributed the first movement of a secular Requiem based on the words of poet Jackie Kay, commissioned for World AIDS Day to benefit Mission Malawi.: *The Moon, My Man and I*. The Halle Orchestra and Chorus premiered this work conducted by Sir Mark Elder, CBE with soloists Roderick Williams and Rebecca Bottone.

His album of his songs, *Secret and Divine Signs* with tenor Michael Slattery received Five Star ratings from the *BBC Music Magazine* and *FM Classic Music Magazine*. Andrew Stewart in *FM Classic Music Magazine* wrote: "... the songs of Urquhart, with their seamless tonal melodies and rippling keyboard accompaniments ... transport the listener into a state of tranquil contemplation by Slattery's sincere delivery."

In reviewing *Calm Seas*, Kathy Parsons for MainlyPiano.com wrote: " I defy anyone to duplicate the soulful, honest, and heartfelt expression Urquhart pours into every note and chord. That's where the magic lies ... you come away feeling that you have gotten to know him rather well - and have perhaps also seen a new facet of your own soul.. it is always a very special experience to be reminded of the power of quiet beauty and simplicity. "

Philip Wharton (ASCAP)

b. 1969

pdwharton@gmail.com
www.philipwharton.com

Few artists enjoy such high praise for both of their disciplines as composer/violinist PHILIP WHARTON. Of his playing, *The New York Times* proclaimed, "a rousing performance!" and *The Waterloo Courier* wrote, "a golden tone with breathtaking execution." His compositions, heralded from coast to coast, are described by the *New York Concert Review* as, "…decidedly contemporary…both engaging and accessible." Writing from symphony to song, past seasons saw the Santa Fe Opera's remounting of *Two Saintes Caught in the Same Act* as part of their apprentice scenes program, the Grammy-nominated Borealis Wind Quintet perform his *Quintet* on their concert tours, his chamber symphony, *Passing Season* performed by regional orchestras, premiere of his *Symphony*, his tribute to Shakespeare's 450th birthday, a song cycle entitled *Fools*, and concerts with Grammy-nominated soprano, Caroline Worra. Other projects include collaborations with author Janet Burroway and illustrator John Vernon Lord to create musical settings of their books for children: *The Giant Jam Sandwich*, *The Truck on the Track*, and a vocal-monodrama, *The Perfect Pig*. Recent recordings include Albany Records' release of his *Flute Sonata*—performed by flutist, Katherine Fink, and pianist Rose Grace, Crescent Phase Records' release of his *Woodwind Quintet*—performed by the Madera Woodwind Quintet, and Kenneth Thompkins' (principal Detroit Symphony Orchestra) recording of his *Alto-Trombone Sonata*. Expect to see the release of a CD by Elizabeth Sombart with the Royal Philharmonic Orchestra in the coming year.

Scott Wheeler (ASCAP)

b. 1952

scott_wheeler@emerson.edu
www.scottwheeler.org

Scott Wheeler's most recent opera is *Naga*, on a libretto of Cerise Jacobs, co-commissioned by White Snake Projects and Boston Lyric Opera. Scott's previous operas have been commissioned by the Metropolitan Opera/Lincoln Center Theatre, Washington National Opera and the Guggenheim Foundation. Scott's 2017 violin sonata, *The Singing Turk*, was commissioned and premiered by Sharan Leventhal, and has been performed many times around the world by Gil Shaham and Akira Eguchi. Other recent works include *200 Dreams from Captivity* for baritone and orchestra on texts of Wang Dan, *Ben Gunn* on texts of Paul Muldoon, and *Nightingale*, a new narrative ballet with choreographer Melissa Barak.

Scott's most recent CDs include *Portraits and Tributes*, featuring pianist Donald Berman, on Bridge, and *Songs to Fill the Void*, featuring baritone Robert Barefield and pianist Carolyn Hague, on Albany. Other Wheeler CDs include *Crazy Weather*, with the Boston Modern Orchestra Project conducted by Gil Rose, *Wasting the Night* -- songs for voice and piano, and the opera *The Construction of Boston*, both available on Naxos; *Shadow Bands* features Scott's chamber music for strings and piano with the Gramercy Trio, recorded on Newport Classic. Scott Wheeler is Senior Distinguished Artist in Residence at Emerson College in Boston, where he teaches musical theatre and songwriting.

Facebook: www.facebook.com/scott.wheeler.52035

David Wolfson (ASCAP)

b. 1964

david@davidwolfsonmusic.net
www.davidwolfsonmusic.net

David Wolfson holds a PhD in composition from Rutgers University, and has taught at Rutgers University, Montclair State University and Hunter College. He is enjoying an eclectic career, having composed opera, musical theatre, touring children's musicals, and incidental music for plays; choral music, band music, orchestral music, chamber music, art songs, and music for solo piano; comedy songs, cabaret songs and one memorable score for an amusement park big-headed-costumed-character show. His CD *Seventeen Windows*, featuring the solo piano suite *Seventeen Windows* and the *Sonata for Cello and Piano*, is available from Albany Records, iTunes and Amazon.com. For more information: www.davidwolfsonmusic.net.

Facebook: www.facebook.com/davidwolfsonmusic/

Roger Zahab (BMI)

b. 1957

www.rogerzahab.net

Roger Zahab instigates complex relations through his activities as composer, violinist, conductor, teacher and writer.

As a violinist, Zahab has given more than a hundred first performances and championed music by a wide range of composers from John Cage to Eric Moe, Kwabena Nketia and Tison Street to Judith Weir and Christian Wolff. Recordings as violinist and composer are available on the Truemedia, Albany and Koch International Classics labels.

Roger is currently Senior Lecturer and Director of the University of Pittsburgh Symphony Orchestra and Music on the Edge Chamber Orchestra, as well as a founding core faculty member of the Vermont College of Fine Arts MFA in Music Composition.

Supplementary Materials

Texts, program notes, composer biographies, and composer headshots can be found at:

https://newmusicshelf.com/anthologies/tenor-v1-info/

www.ingramcontent.com/pod-product-compliance
Lightning Source LLC
Chambersburg PA
CBHW080343170426
43194CB00014B/2664